Monumental Minnesota

Monumental Minnesota

A GUIDE TO
OUTDOOR SCULPTURE

Moira F. Harris

ISBN 9617767-9-X.

Library of Congress Catalogue Card No. 91–50931.

Cover photograph: St. Urho, the Patron Saint of the
Vintners of Finland. Crafted in fiberglass. Located in Menahga, Minnesota.

Chapter drawings by Bill Stein.

Contents

Preface

Monumental Minnesota is a wish-book for any art lover with catholic tastes and gasoline feet. Its topic is serious business. Minnesotans put their values out at the crossroads when they place a work of art in a public, corporate or institutional setting. Widely known as reticent citizens, Minnesotans nonetheless erect bold statements of their ideals, aspirations, and sense of humor for all the world to see. Many outdoor sculptures are high-minded expressions of officially sanctioned taste and shared community beliefs. But outdoor sculpture is also an outlaw art form that revels in its aesthetic excesses. It is an art form that can thumb its concrete, fiberglass or chain-sawn nose at the pronouncements of artworld experts and selection committees. Minnesota's outdoor sculpture can claim for its two Muses an allegorical figure in chaste marble on the State Capitol, and a thirty foot fiberglass Mermaid on a suburban supper club.

There is plenty of literature on outdoor sculpture in America, with its own web of cross-reference through art history, American studies, folklife, and conservation. Monumental Minnesota draws from and gives to all these scholarly specialties in its wealth of insights. But it has an essential ingredient too many writings on the topic lack: an unquenchable enthusiasm to match its solid research. You will find Monumental Minnesota an essential tool to enrich your travels on Minnesota's blue highways. When you are on the road and hungry for sights more stimulating than cafes and water towers, this book will show you where to look for hundreds of sculptures. When you come upon an abstract steel assemblage or a prairie chicken the size of a Dairy Queen, this book will tell you what you are looking at, why it is there, and what it has meant to its community.

Monumental Minnesota will tempt you to browse its pages on dreary weekday nights at home. Search it for a Sunday drive that will take you from point A to point B, by way of sculptural detours to the sublime and the outrageous. It will earn a place on your bookshelves with the WPA Guide To Minnesota, Karal Ann Marling's Colossus of Roads, and David Gebhard and Tom Martinson's Guide To The Architecture of Minnesota. But use this book on the road, too. I am sure Ms. Harris will take no offense if you stash it in the glove compartment, scribble in the margins, or spill Kwik-Stop coffee on its cover. She has put the key to the highway in your hands. Fill your tank and go forth, in search of Minnesota's most generous and unabashed art form.

Thomas O'Sullivan
Curator of Art
Minnesota Historical Society

Introduction

When the research for *Monumental Minnesota* began, an explanation of the project brought interesting responses: "Is there anything outside of the Twin Cities?" or "How will you find the statues?" Three years, some 630 statues and 150 towns later, it is very clear that Minnesota towns have sculpture. Plenty of it, in fact. Finding it was sometimes easy, sometimes hard, and often serendipitous. My published guides were the books which Tom O'Sullivan mentions in the Preface. My other sources were far more numerous. There were the usual archival sources: the libraries in Minneapolis, St. Paul, the University of Minnesota, the Walker Art Center and the Minnesota Historical Society. Artists, arts administrators, and archivists at county historical societies and even passersby all supplied leads. One day, for example, while I was photographing Dennis Roghair's "Statue of Liberty" in Milaca a woman stopped to ask if I knew "where the others were?" This was the lead to further works by Roghair in Milaca and Onamia.

The goal was to locate, identify and document as many sculptures as possible. From the beginning my limitations were only those of location and ownership. Was the sculpture outdoors and on permanent public view in Minnesota? There are many debates, of course, over what is and what is not "public art." For this guide sculpture which is generally accessible to the public at convenient times is considered "public." Anything located indoors is excluded from the listing. "Privately owned" is a more problematic limitation. Clearly businesses, museums, hospitals, colleges and universities, and occasionally churches, all commission and display art. These are often private institutions yet I have generally included them because their display of outdoor sculpture is for the public to see and enjoy. What I have generally excluded are sculptures located at private residences, with the exception of the folk art environments discussed in Chapter Seven.

Defining what is a piece of sculpture is probably the most difficult task. Once it was easy. A sculpture was made of stone, metal, glass or wood. It either stood by itself on a base or was attached to a building. Critics and artists were equally sure what sculpture was. F. A. Gutheim wrote in 1933 that "the fundamental justification on which all civic sculpture rests is the commemoration of present and past persons and events for future generations. Public statues often become more; they memorialize the dominant taste of a period even more strikingly than other arts . . . " (Gutheim 1933). And Harry Rand cited Paul Manship's three pronged theory of monuments given in his notebooks:

A monument should be permanent . . . A monument should be fit for high moral and devotional purposes . . . A monument should be beautiful. (Rand 1989: 167).

Probably many artists and the public in Minnesota before 1930 would have agreed with those premises. Chapter One ("Early Heroes") describes civic sculptures which commemorate people and events in just the manner Gutheim advocated.

As sculpture became more abstract or experimental and was created from new materials the definitions of what sculpture is had to expand. Robert Goldwater's book, *What is Modern Sculpture?* (1969) gave the following stylistic classifications: Impressionism, Symbolism, Cubism, Futurism, Dada, Surrealism, Biomorphism, Constructivism, and Assemblage. There were more "isms" to come; examples of most if not all of these sculptural styles can be found in the Minneapolis Sculpture Garden.

In Chapter Four (which deals with the public art programs supported by federal, state, or local monies) sculpture ranging from pedestal and relief works of the 1930's to Percent for Art Programs since 1983 is described. *The Policies and Procedures of the Minnesota Percent for Art in Public Places Program* (updated version, August 10, 1990) defines artworks as original and unique creations. Three dimensional sculpture includes "Work in relief, in the round, assemblages, constructions, environments including landscaping, and other permanent installations in any materials or combination of materials." Artworks can include "building or landscape features such as gates, streetlights, floors, seating, etc. in unique or limited editions produced under the control of an artist" (*Policies and Procedures* 1990: 3). As the Listing of Outdoor Sculpture indicates, Minnesota's artists are creating walkways, seatings, gates, manhole covers, skyways, and bridges, as well as the traditional pedestal, relief and fountain sculptures. The bemused account of a recent San Francisco conference on public art began, "The most important popular criteria for public art is: Can you sit on it?" (*San Francisco Chronicle*, November 19, 1991).

Statisticians can probably use the Listing of Outdoor Sculpture to discover the oldest or newest works, the most popular subjects or materials, or the names of artists, but the first outdoor sculpture in Minnesota is not listed. The "Angel Gabriel" was made in 1854 in Lyons, France, for display at a New York exposition. Captain James Winslow purchased the angel from a trader in La Crosse, Wisconsin, and brought the eight foot long gilded bronze to Minnesota in 1857. When the Winslow House was completed in St. Anthony the work was placed on a flagpole outside the hotel's main entrance. In 1938 Merle Potter wrote that "the settlers for miles around came to view the figure as though it were the eighth wonder of the world. Probably right there began the interest that was later to produce a Walker art gallery and the Minneapolis Institute of Arts. At any rate it is true that St. Anthony had this object of European art in its midst before it had a railroad" (*Minneapolis Tribune,* September 28, 1938). The "Angel Gabriel" (which was a weather vane) continued to show the way the wind was blowing in front of Winslow House until 1886. Then the old hotel was wrecked and replaced by the Minneapolis Exposition Building. The tower of that building was the new location for the weather vane until 1939, when the wrecker's ball appeared. The "Angel Gabriel" was saved once again and can now be viewed on a high, dark wall of the Museum of the Hennepin County Historical Society in Minneapolis.

Many Minnesota sculptures have been photographed for use on postcards. Such city views have been popular since the birth of the picture postcards in the 1890's. A postcard image can indicate that a statue once existed and, in the case of Rochester's "Abraham Lincoln," that can begin a search. A postcard in the Audio Visual Library of the Minnesota Historical Society showed this statue of President Lincoln with the caption "City Park, Rochester" and a postmark dated 1915. On visits to Rochester no such statue could be located although the name "Statuary Parking Lot" was a clue to what had once existed. Clippings in the library of the Olmsted County Historical Society provided part of the story. In 1910 the city of Rochester was given two marble

statues by the Doctors William and Charles Mayo. On Memorial Day, 1911, statues of Lincoln and Washington were dedicated in Mayo Park. The statues were carved in Florence, Italy, by Antonio Frilli. (M. H. de Young bought a similar pair from the Panama Pacific Exposition in 1915 for his museum in San Francisco.) Until 1938 Rochester's Lincoln and Washington statues stood in Mayo Park with a cannon separating them. Then vandals using a crowbar tipped the statues over. The right arm was broken, the nose chipped, and the entire figure of Lincoln pried loose from its pedestal; only a chipped nose was suffered by Washington. Indignation was expressed by various civic groups and eventually the statues were repaired (*Rochester Post-Bulletin,* March 28, 1938). They remained in the Park until 1954 when the City decided it needed parking lots more than the statues. Washington and Lincoln were then sent to a Parks Department storage warehouse, and that building burned in 1966. The remains of the building and presumably the statues were taken to a landfill. The Frilli statues are now many feet below a freeway, according to Warren Throndson, a retired Parks Department employee.

During the research and writing of *Monumental Minnesota,* sculpture has often been in the news. Lacking barricades and Bastilles to storm, crowds in Eastern Europe have toppled Lenin, Dzerzhinsky, Stalin, Enver Hoxha, Molotov, and Yakov Sverdlov. Rather than a sculpture garden, Moscow now has a heap of dismembered figures near Gorky Park with a sign identifying them as "sculptures of the servants of the totalitarian regime" (*The New York Times,* September 4, 1991). Correspondents reporting from Baghdad during the Desert Storm campaign occasionally stood near a giant arch formed by colossal reproductions of Saddam Hussein's forearms. A short, but amazing book called *The Monument* (1991) by Samir al-Khalil describes this incredible Iraqi colossus. All Minnesotans don't regard all Minnesota outdoor sculptures with pleasure. There is vandalism, there is outrage, and as sculptor Kent Nerburn discovered when he dared to critize Bemidji's "Paul Bunyan and Babe the Blue Ox" there is genuine affection for very large concrete effigies (*St. Paul Pioneer Press*, January 5 and March 2, 1990.) But after the first flurry of columns or letters to the editor, outdoor sculpture is usually allowed to remain and, more than likely, be ignored. Yet, to forget what towns and cities have on display is a mistake. This book provides a record of the sculpture seen in outdoor Minnesota in 1991, and is meant to serve as a guide to the state's artistic heritage.

With only a few exceptions (art in the towns of Baudette and Embarass, and soon to be installed on the Nicollet Mall and Duluth's Canal Park) the sculpture which I have listed I have seen and photographed. Sculpture dimensions sometimes had to be approximated if no published or accurate source existed. In the listing dimensions are given in the customary manner with height first followed by width and depth. Dimensions of some complex and composite sculptures with many parts are simply summarized as "various." Dating is given in the following manner: an original work created for the place where it is still located has one date. If a work (Houdon's "George Washington" for example) exists in many copies I have given the original date, followed by "c" for the year in which it was cast. A work which has been moved has a letter "m" preceding the date.

Some of the artworks in this guide have often been the subject of photographs. For example in 1990 Walker Art Center published a catalogue of its collection, so it seemed redundant to use photographs of the works in the Minneapolis Sculpture Garden or on the Walker Art Center terraces. What I have selected, instead, are photographs of works which may not be as familiar and these are, unless otherwise noted, my own photographs.

In compiling this record I am indebted to many people for their insight and assistance. My father, John T. Flanagan, my husband John, and daughter Cecily accompanied me on some of the research trips. I was grateful for their company and understanding. Others who guided me to find what I needed to know include Regina Flanagan, Bob Booker, Jack Becker, Jan Marlese, Tom O'Sullivan, Dave Nystuen, Claire Martin, Stewart Turnquist, Ann Stout, Don McNeil, Gretchen Finnerty, Lee Bjorklund, Mrs. Doad Schroeder, Marlyce Nygard, Michael Conforti, Karen Duncan, and Leann Klein. In addition to the libraries listed above I was able to consult the archives of "Celebrate Minnesota 1990"; the Historic Sites Survey at Fort Snelling; the files of the Minneapolis Arts Commmission, the St. Paul Department of Parks and Recreation, and the Nicollet Mall Implementation Board; as well as the college archives at Concordia (Moorhead), Gustavus Adolphus, Carleton, St. Catherine's, St. John's and the University of St. Thomas. Staffs of the Dakota, Hennepin, Otter Tail, Freeborn, Kandiyohi, Winona, Goodhue, McLeod, Pipestone, Mower, Lyon, Big Stone and Stearns County Historical Societies were especially helpful.

At times the key to identification of sculpture was located in local newspapers. Knowing when a sculpture was dedicated provided the clue to locating a news story. However, the saddest words I often heard were that the newspaper was on microfilm, but that there was no index. I thank John Bloomquist of the *Menahga-Sebeka Review Messenger* for his file on St. Urho; the Chambers of Commerce at Crosby, Madison, Olivia, Two Harbors, Hibbing, Virginia, and Baudette; city employees of Cloquet, Cambridge, Big Fork and Silver Bay; and librarians at Grand Marais, Blue Earth, Duluth, St. Cloud, and Owatonna, all of whom provided useful information.

Lastly, but far from least, I wish to thank the many artists who told me about their works and, where desired, provided permission to use photographs of their works, including but not limited to Evelyn Raymond, Charles Gagnon, Michael Price, Paul Granlund, Stewart Luckman, Stanton Sears, Chuck Huntington, Anthony Caponi, Andrew Leicester, Douglas Freeman, Bruce Stillman, Nick Legeros, Georgette Sosin, Seitu Jones, Rodger Brodin, George Bassett, Norman Holen, Russell Erickson, Robert Johnson, Robert Ed, Jon Strom, Jerry Vettrus, Mary Degen, Ray Wattenhofer, Dennis Weimar, Larry Jensen, Jerry Faber, Dennis Roghair and Arnold Gruter.

Moira F. Harris
St. Paul, Minnesota
December 17, 1991.

Just the place for a statue, the Artist said
　　As he sketched his idea with chalk.
In a pool with a fountain my marble mountain
　　Will cause all the people to talk.
They'll come for miles, view it with smiles
　　And agree from the depths of their hearts
That it's providential it's so monumental
　　But best of all they've seen Art!
　　　　　　　　　　Anon.

1   Early Heroes

Before 1900, with the notable exception of Jakob Fjelde's work, most of Minnesota's outdoor sculpture was created by artists who lived somewhere else. Pedestals and bases were often carved of Minnesota granite by local stone masons, but the heroic figure on top was modelled or cast by a sculptor in another state or country.

Even commercial signs were obtained elsewhere. In 1891 the New York Life Insurance Company supplied a new three dimensional logo for its office building at Minnesota and Sixth Streets in St. Paul. The logo shows a bronze eagle landing on a rock ledge with a snake in its talons for the hungry eaglets to devour. This patriotic and nurturing emblem was designed by Louis St. Gaudens and cast at least twice more for company offices in Omaha and Kansas City. Eagle and eaglets survived the demolition of the company's building in 1967 and now rest on a pedestal in front of a parking ramp at Jackson and Fourth Streets.

Wooden shop signs once were common in most towns and cities, perhaps due to the verbal but not visual illiteracy of the population. Wooden boots, metal eyeglasses, and painted mortar and pestles all hung above doorways to indicate what a shop sold. Best known of these signs were the Cigar Store Indians, painted figures of wood or metal which welcomed customers to the world of tobacco from a place on the sidewalk in front

One of downtown St. Paul's important monuments is Louis St. Gaudens' "New York Eagle" (1891). Once located high above the insurance company's doorway, the eagle now offers its young a taste of snake outside a parking ramp.

of the store. Jean Lipman pointed out that, although Indian figures were used in seventeenth century England, it was not until the mid-nineteenth century that such shop signs became popular in America. "The heyday of the Indian was from the fifties through the eighties," Lipman wrote (Lipman, 1948: 73). In his small book on the Minnesota town of Red Wing Laurence Schmeckebier included a photograph of a typical wooden Indian once in use by the Nelson store (Schmeckebier 1946: 67). Another Indian figure spent sixty years on a sidewalk in downtown Stillwater and undoubtedly a number of others were familiar sights in the life of many Minnesota Main Streets.

One Indian figure, however, led a rather traumatic life, and is still located outside although far from any cigar store. Originally on view in front of the Chapman Cigar Store in St. Paul the painted zinc alloy figure was sold to several collectors before becoming the property of J. L. Shiely in 1948. Mr. Shiely placed the painted Indian in a small garden behind his gravel company on North Snelling Avenue, where it remained for several years more. In 1958 the Indian was

As he slowly revolves on a turntable, the "Indian Scout" (c1900) gazes alternately down the Mississippi River and then into the restaurant of the Pool and Yacht Club in Lilydale. Once he held a bow and arrows outside a St. Paul cigar store, but his tobacco days are now done.

dubbed a Scout and was placed on a base in Lily-dale, overlooking the junction of the Minnesota and Mississippi Rivers. Officials of the D.A.R. and the Minnesota Historical Society participated in a ceremony honoring the Indian's new role. Unfortunately vandals, using a battering ram, severely damaged the figure the following year. Less than a month after it was repaired and replaced it was kidnapped and repositioned, to direct traffic at Cleveland and Randolph Streets, near the College of St. Catherine (*St. Paul Pioneer Press*, August 13, 1958; June 30, 1959; and August 11, 1959). Returned once more to Lilydale, the Indian now stands watch on the deck of the Pool and Yacht Club, just off Highway 13.

Folk art specialist Frederick Fried wrote that this Indian was the most popular of the metal cigar store figures. Based on a wooden figure carved by Samuel Robb of New York, the metal version was copyrighted by William Demuth and Company, also of New York, in 1872. Fried illustrates a catalogue page from the Demuth Company in which the Indian appears with feathers in his headband and carrying a bow and arrows (Fried 1970: 54). In Pittsburgh a similar figure was purchased by H. J. Heinz from the J. L. Mott Iron Works in 1896. It is known as "Guyasuta" in honor of a Seneca chief who had known George Washington. Marilyn Evert noted that most of the twenty Indian Chief figures located thus far have names honoring local Indians. Some, like Pittsburgh's "Guyasuta," and a figure sometimes called "Atahuallpa" given to the city of Cuzco, Peru, were purchased as fountain centerpieces, rather than as trade signs (Evert 1983: 335–337).

Many of Minnesota's Beaux-arts style county court houses built around the turn of the last century were designed with a dome whose proper finial was a figure of Justice. Blindfolded Justice usually carries scales in one hand and a sword in the other. At least a few of these Justice figures can still be seen *in situ* on court houses at Pipestone, Bemidji and Windom. The State's second Capitol building, demolished in 1939, also had a Justice figure on its dome. That figure, of painted metal plates welded over a carved tree trunk, is now in the collections of the McLeod County Historical Society in Hutchinson. T. D. Allen, the architect of the Steele County Court House in Owatonna, varied the format by designing a niche for a trio of "Mercy, Justice and Law" placed over the entrance of that building. The figures are made of lightweight metal welded together and then gilded. Most Justice figures are obviously difficult either to see or to photograph, but one formerly located on the Cass County Court House now stands at ground level next to the county's historical museum in Walker. This Justice figure is dated 1902 and was given to the museum in 1961.

Dating from the same period as the Justice figures is Alfonso Pelzer's statue of "Hermann the Cheruscan," who triumphantly holds court atop a domed temple in New Ulm. The actual Hermann, or Arminius (c18 B.C.–19 A.D.), was a Germanic chief who led his people in battle against the Romans and defeated a force of three Roman legions in 9 A.D. The legendary hero was honored in 1876 with a temple and statue near Detmold, Germany, in the Teutoberg forest, near the scene of his victory over the Romans. By the 1880's there were 362 lodges of a fraternal group called the Sons of Hermann in the United States, including 53 lodges in Minnesota, and there was a clear interest in building America's monument to Hermann. Julius Berndt persuaded the organization to sponsor such a monument (which he designed) on land he owned in New Ulm. Work began on Berndt's unusual temple in 1887. Its culminating 32 foot tall Hermann statue was fashioned of copper sheet sections in Salem, Ohio, and then shipped to New Ulm in 1890. The entire monument was dedicated on September 25, 1897. The Hermann monument is listed on both the state and national Registers of Historic Sites.

Thus, when Jakob Fjelde arrived in Minneapolis in 1887 he did not have many competitors or colleagues as sculptors. Most sculpture in Minnesota at the time was not created locally, as architects and contractors were probably accustomed to placing these commissions elsewhere. It took years to change that habit, but the work of Fjelde certainly gave it a start. Jakob Fjelde was born in Norway and trained as a sculptor there and in Italy. In Minneapolis he completed portrait busts including a head of the city's founder, Colonel John H. Stevens. In 1893 he submitted a plaster model of the Hiawatha and Minnehaha characters from the poem by Henry Wadsworth Longfellow to be displayed in the Minnesota building at the World's Columbian Exposition in Chicago. A Mankato woman, Mrs. L. P. Hunt, led a fundraising campaign so that a bronze cast of "Hiawatha and Minnehaha" could be placed by Minnehaha Creek in Minneapolis. Fjelde did not live to see the dedication of this work in 1912 nor of his bronze figure of "Ole Bull" (1810–1880) in Loring Park in 1897. Bull, the famous Norwegian violinist, had made concert appearances in Minnesota so that this subject was a welcome one for local Norwegian-Americans and other music lovers. That figure was dedicated on Syttende Mai (Norwegian Independence Day) in Minneapolis' Loring Park, where it still can be seen.

Fjelde's other outdoor works have not always remained in their original locations. His over life-size figure of "Minerva" (1889) stood above the entrance to the Minneapolis Public Library at 10th Street and Hennepin Avenue until that building was demolished. "Minerva" now inspires learning inside the new Downtown Library at 4th Street and Hennepin Avenue. The bronze statue of "Colonel Stevens," a gift from his daughter to the city of Minneapolis in 1912, was first located at Grant Street and Portland Avenue South, but it was moved to Minnehaha Park near the Stevens home (which had also been moved from its original location) in 1935. The statue was completed by J. S. Gelert, using Fjelde's bust of Stevens as the model for the head. The twenty-four spandrel reliefs Fjelde designed can still be seen on Burton Hall at the East Bank Campus of the University of Minnesota, but his bronze bust of Henrik Ibsen was stolen from its pedestal in St. Paul's Como Park in 1981 and never found.

Outdoor sculpture is often relocated and the new location is not always a felicitous choice. Artists design their work to take advantage of the terrain and sight lines, and when a work is moved those aspects of the statue's impact on the viewer may be destroyed. The saga of Winona's "Princess Wenonah" is a case in point. William J. Landon commissioned this work in 1900 as a memorial to his late wife. The artist selected was Isabel Moore Kimball, a young Iowa woman who had studied at the Art Institute of Chicago, with Lorado Taft at his Midway Studios, and at the Pratt Institute of Brooklyn with Herbert Adams. Miss Kimball taught in Minnesota for several years and for one summer she served as a drawing instructor at the Winona Teacher's College.

The Landon memorial (unveiled in 1902) took the form of a spacious fountain. The bronze statue of "Princess Wenonah" stood in the center on a granite pedestal around whose base were three bronze pelicans. From the rim of the forty foot basin three bronze snapping turtles directed water back at the pelicans. The fountain was designed for Central Square, where it stood for sixty years. When that land was needed for a new post office building the figure of "Princess Wenonah" was sent to Main and Lake Streets while her pelicans and turtles went first into storage and then to the campus of Winona State University. In 1977 all were reunited in the city's Levee Plaza Mall. "Princess Wenonah," her pelicans and turtles, are now tightly arranged on a rock pile over which water flows.

Miss Kimball sought to avoid in her work the criticism which Jakob Fjelde had received over the authenticity of his "Hiawatha and Minnehaha" figures and, especially, over their seemingly European features. Several Indian girls posed for the artist in her Brooklyn studio while the treatment of the Sioux dress, hair style and ornaments was based on museum examples (*Winona Daily Republican and Herald,* August 6, 1902). The "Princess Wenonah" fountain was Isabel Moore Kimball's only Minnesota work, and it is considered to be her most important sculpture.

Funding of many outdoor sculptures at this time was by individual gifts, like that of Landon, by a committee assembled for the sole purpose of commissioning a monument, or through the efforts of fraternal lodges, patriotic groups, or

Jakob Fjelde's "Ole Bull" (1897) was given to the city of Minneapolis by a committee of Norwegian-Americans. The sculpture stands in Loring Park.

veteran's organizations. A Swedish-American committee raised funds for the statue of the Swedish writer and educator, Gunnar Wennerberg (1817–1901) in Minneapolis' Minnehaha Park, while a German-American group in St. Paul worked to finance a statue in Como Park, honoring the German poet, Johann Christoph Friedrich von Schiller (1759–1805). A file of the correspondence and newspaper accounts relating to the Schiller statue includes an interesting view of the problems which that committee faced (*Schiller Monument Committee Papers*, Minnesota Historical Society Archives).

The cornerstone was placed in Como Park in 1905 on the centenary of Schiller's death, but it would be two more years before the standing bronze statue and its granite pedestal were ready for dedication. The Committee was led by Ferdinand Willius, and its other members were brewers Otto Bremer and William Hamm, Hugo Hanft, the city's Health Commissioner Dr. Justus Ohage and the German Consul Hans Grunow. As a number of Schiller statues already existed in both America and Europe, so at first the committee thought of having a copy made. That idea was rejected when it was learned that if no mold had been kept a sculptor would have to be hired to make a new original. And, as Karl Bitter wrote to Chairman Willius, no American sculptor of any repute would be willing to make such a copy (Letter, September 3, 1905).

The committee consulted Cass Gilbert, the architect of the Minnesota State Capitol Building, who replied that the proposed monument "should be beautiful and appropriate. If it is not beautiful it is worse than none at all. Bad art has no excuse for existence and cheap reproductions of commonplace designs, no matter where else they may have been erected, are to be avoided out of civic pride if for no other reason" (Letter, December 4, 1905). Gilbert had also been asked to suggest names of sculptors, perhaps resident in Minnesota or of German-descent, and to that he responded, "I am bound to confess my ignorance as to the existence of any artist residing in St. Paul who has demonstrated a sufficient reputation to justify the placing of an important statue in his hands. This is a question of art and not a question of locality. Artists are found where there is most opportunity for their endeavor" (Letter, December 4, 1905).

The committee also consulted the Austrian-born sculptor Karl Bitter as to whether a European artist would make a better choice. Bitter, who had directed the sculptural programs at the St. Louis World's Fair and the Pan-American Exposition in Buffalo and knew American sculptors well, was not totally in agreement. He wrote frankly to committee chairman Willius, "It appears that foreign sculptors consider American commissions as so-called pot boilers and fear little harm to their reputations by doing negligent

Harriet Hanley's statue of "George Wright" (1926) was a gift from his son to the city of Fergus Falls. Wright was a surveyor so that is how he is dressed for the monument on Union Avenue.

work for a community which they believe notorious for its lack of artistic appreciation" (Letter, September 21, 1905). Eventually the committee members wrote to Karl Marr, a Milwaukee-born professor of art at the University of Munich. Marr provided a sketch of Schiller which then became a heroic size statue done by Ignatius Taschner. The selected sculptor worked in wood and bronze, and was also a painter, printmaker, book illustrator and graphic designer. The resulting "Schillerdenkmal" was almost ten feet in height standing upon a pedestal of Vermont granite and cost about $6,000. The statue was unveiled in Como Park on July 7, 1907, with speeches and music by German singing societies and the Frank Danz band (*St. Paul Daily Pioneer Press*, July 8, 1907).

The early heroes were followed by statues of politicians, city founders, and explorers. The statue of Minneapolis' city founder John H. Stevens has already been noted. In Fergus Falls a 20 foot tall granite tribute to George B. Wright (1835–1882), surveyor and town founder, stands in a small park along Union Avenue. The inscription on the granite pedestal reads:

> Surveyor, Versatile Businessman who Founded Fergus Falls A. D. 1870 who promoted its interests, took part in its early activities and controvercies (sic) and whose Faith in "The Coming City" lent an impetus which endures.

Wright is shown wearing a fringed buckskin jacket embroidered in silk which had been a favorite garment in his surveying days.

The Wright statue was the work of Harriet Hanley, a Minneapolis sculptor who is far better known for her career as an art gallery owner. Needing a job after her husband became seriously ill she went to work at first selling prints in Mabel Ulrich's bookstore on Nicollet Avenue in Minneapolis, and then opened her own art gallery. An article by Margaret Morris noted that she discovered artists, helped build their reputations, "and made the city art conscious" (*Minneapolis Tribune*, April 8, 1951). At the time of her death in 1962, art critic John K. Sherman paid tribute to her faultless good taste and quiet determination in exhibiting quality art, and in making sure that there was a place where the work of Minnesota artists could be seen (*Minneapolis Sunday Tribune*, November 4, 1962).

As Rochester is synonymous with the Mayo Clinic, it is not surprising to find statues of the Doctors Mayo in Mayo Park. The statue of William Worrall Mayo (1819–1911), the initiator of this medical tradition, is the work of Leonard Crunelle. Lorado Taft wrote of Crunelle that "Circumstances compel him to model soldier memorials and dead governors in Prince Albert coats" (Taft 1930: 583), although the artist was far more skilled at depicting the emotions of babies and children. Dr. Mayo, in his tightly buttoned Prince Albert coat, looks seriously towards the city from his pedestal on Second Avenue.

One of many artworks given to the city of Rochester by the Mayo family is this figure of "William Worrall Mayo" (1911) by Leonard Crunelle.

In contrast to the statue of their father (who is seen in an overcoat), "The Doctors Mayo" (1952) pose as if they had just left the operating room. Their double portrait by James Earle Fraser is located in Rochester's Mayo Park in front of the Civic Center.

Nearby, wearing surgical gowns, stand his sons, Dr. William J. (1861–1939) and Dr. Charles H. (1865–1939). Their over lifesize portrait in bronze is the work of Winona-born sculptor James Earle Fraser. Fraser is best known for his "End of the Trail" statue first exhibited at the Panama Pacific Exposition in 1915 and for his designs for the United States Buffalo nickel coin. In 1964 the United States post office issued a five cent postage stamp in "surgical green" honoring the Doctors Mayo, whose design is based on the heads from the Fraser monument seen in profile.

In an open courtyard at St. Marys Hospital in Rochester is a bronze statue of Edith Graham Mayo (1867–1943), the work of her granddaughter, Mayo Kooiman. Edith Mayo, the wife of Dr. Charles H. Mayo, was the first trained nurse in Rochester and is shown hurrying on her medical rounds. Complementing these serious images of the Mayos at work is "The Mothers" (1978) a lighthearted bronze group by Paul T. Granlund, located in Louise Park in Le Sueur. The Park is named for the two women who occupied the house next door, Louise Mayo (William Worrall's wife) and Louise Cosgrove (wife and mother of Green Giant Company presidents). The two Louises stand with hands touching as three of their children skip underneath the encircling arms in a typical Granlund composition of touching and turning figures.

Returning to St. Paul and its growing group of heroes on the Capitol Mall, it is appropriate

to mention the great white building at the top of the hill, Cass Gilbert's State Capitol, completed in 1905. Minnesotans had erected two earlier capitol buildings. The original, finished in 1853, burned in 1881. A new market house constructed by the city of St. Paul at Seventh and Wabasha streets, was then offered to the State for its use and served in that capacity until no longer needed. A second capitol, built in 1883, was in use until Cass Gilbert's structure was completed in 1905. (This was the building which once had a figure of Justice on its dome, and was demolished in 1939.) Gilbert's design, which William Watts Folwell wrote had "sufficient but not superfluous, decorative elements" (Folwell 1926: III, 269) does have significant exterior sculpture. Marble eagles guard the dome and marble figures stand guard duty along the loggia, but it is the gleaming gilded quadriga called "Progress of the State" which is the focus of attention. Gilbert selected Daniel Chester French to design the sculpture for the building and especially to create a quadriga such as the one French and Edward Potter, the animal sculptor, had exhibited at the World's Columbian Exhibition in Chicago. "Progress of the State" included a chariot with a standing rider, four prancing horses and two walking figures. All were fashioned of copper sheets hammered over steel frames, then gilded. The charioteer (Man) proceeds towards the State's goals of progress and prosperity, carrying a horn of plenty in his right arm and holding aloft a banner marked "Minnesota" in his left. The forces of Nature are embodied by the prancing horses who are controlled by the two women who represent Civilization. Below the "Progress of the State" quadriga are six marble figures illustrating wisdom, courage, bounty, prudence, truth and integrity. Among the sculptors who came to Minnesota to work at the Capitol was Albert Corwin. Several of the eagles and two of the female loggia figures were among his work.

French received another local commission in 1900 while he was working on the quadriga. This was for a portrait statue of Governor John S. Pillsbury (1827–1901), which faces Burton Hall, on the East Bank Campus of the University of Minnesota. Pillsbury, called the "father of the University of Minnesota," had been very involved with the development of the Minneapolis campus as a member of the University's Board of Regents, so that the location for the monument was quite appropriate. French placed a standing figure of the Governor on a small pedestal in front of a curving wall with benches. The Governor gestures, as if making a point. Pillsbury attended the Monument's dedication, whose program was preserved in a small volume printed for the occasion.

Three Minnesota governors (John A. Johnson, Floyd B. Olson, and Knute Nelson) have been remembered in sculptures placed on the Capitol Mall. Johnson's statue was the first and the campaign for its realization was quite different from that for any other memorial. John Albert Johnson was born near St. Peter (a town which happily calls itself the birthplace of governors) in 1861, the son of Swedish immigrants. He had to leave school at the age of thirteen to help support his mother, the village's washerwoman. At twenty-five he became editor of the *St. Peter Herald* and within a dozen years was elected to the state legislature. Johnson proved to be a good campaigner and was elected Governor as a Democrat in 1904 when Republicans were winning all other state offices. He was re-elected in 1906 and 1908 and there began to be hints that Johnson might be presidential material. Clearly he could speak well and apparently enjoyed campaign appearances and lectures on the Chautauqua circuit. After a lecture in Urbana, Illinois, in August of 1909 he became ill and less than one month later he was dead. Cyrus Northrup, then president of the University of Minnesota, wrote that "The mourning over his untimely death has hardly been equalled by the mourning for any other citizen except Abraham Lincoln" (Folwell 1926: III, 283). A Johnson memorial commission was quickly appointed by Governor Adolf Eberhardt, who succeeded Johnson in office. Records of the Johnson memorial commission are in the Archives of the Minnesota Historical Society.

From the beginning it was determined that anyone who wished to contribute could do so, but no one could give more than one dollar. Information about the memorial was printed by newspapers in every town. Contributions and lists of their donors came from the entire state with the exception of St. Peter whose citizens planned to have their own memorial. At first the committee hoped for at least eight to ten thousand dollars which would pay for a marble statue, but with a total of $23,950.04 raised, their vision turned to bronze.

The committee decided to assemble a list of well regarded sculptors and then invite them to submit information about their work. That plan didn't prevent others from suggesting artists or sculptors from asking if they could be considered. Paul Manship wrote to C. D. O'Brien, president of the commission:

. . . that it would be the opportunity of my life to design the monument to our great governor. I might say here that should I receive the award of this commission I should give up the American Prix de

Rome which I am now holding to devote all necessary attention to the desired results.
(Letter, November 18, 1909.)

O'Brien replied that he couldn't be included in their short list of candidates "as your reputation is still to be made" (Letter, January 20, 1910). Manship, by the nineteen twenties one of America's most successful sculptors, never did receive a commission for an outdoor portrait figure in Minnesota. His only outdoor work was a fountain group called "Indian Hunter and his Dog" (1926), created for a small park on Summit Avenue in St. Paul.

After due deliberation the committee selected Andrew O'Connor to create their monument for Governor Johnson. After O'Connor had reviewed photographs and articles about Johnson as well as the death mask of the Governor by Paul Manship, the sculptor wrote to C. W. Ames, the committee secretary:

He was so simple, so sad and so evidently suffering that his statue must have these elements before all others and I shall try to make this statue as much like him as possible.
(Letter, May 20, 1910.)

Ames quickly replied that:

Johnson certainly did have something of the Lincoln quality, but if you emphasize the melancholy side of his nature and make a man of sorrows of him, you will not present him as we knew him. He had a cheerful, healthy nature, serious indeed, but not sad.
(Letter, May 31, 1910.)

O'Connor completed two Lincoln statues in the years to come: a standing figure called "Lincoln of the Farewell Address" (1918) in front of the Illinois State House in Springfield, and a seated figure (1922) located in Fort Lincoln Ceme-

Only a few of Minnesota's governors have been remembered in outdoor sculptures. Andrew O'Connor's figure of "John A. Johnson" (1912) was created first for the Capitol Mall in St. Paul and then repeated in a simpler version for St. Peter. This figure, dedicated in 1913, stands next to the Nicollet County Court House in St. Peter.

tery, Maryland. Both figures have rather melancholy expressions.

By October O'Connor had sent sketches to St. Paul and there was a firestorm of disapproval. The committee didn't like the face or the coat the figure wore, and the chairman of the committee did not approve of a frieze of allegorical figures which the sculptor had suggested for the pedestal. Secretary Ames wrote to the artist that typical figures of Minnesota industries should stand at the corners of the pedestal. Most of all, Ames wrote, the committee was concerned; "Can O'Connor make Johnson as we knew him?" (Letter, November 8, 1910).

Eventually the artist submitted bronze pedestal models of a farmer, miner, and iron worker which were accepted, but his timber cruiser needed more work. As Ames wrote to O'Connor:

These men never carry their packs by a bandage on their heads, but by straps over their arms.
(Letter, December 11, 1911.)

In January of 1912 photographs of Leonidas Merritt were sent and the artist was advised to make his timber cruiser resemble Merritt (Letter from Ames, January 15, 1912). It had been a long process, but eventually the Johnson Monument was completed and officially dedicated on October 19, 1912. The committee had approved of the expression, the clothing and, last of all, the timber cruiser figure.

For St. Peter's monument, O'Connor made a copy of the figure of Governor Johnson, but the pedestal was lower and lacked its four smaller bronze figures. Dedication of that monument took place in 1913, on the fourth anniversary of the Governor's death, in the small park to the east of the Nicollet County Court house.

Karl Bitter had offered to do a Schiller statue for St. Paul, and had been considered for the

JOHN ALBERT JOHNSON
1861   1909
BORN IN ST. PETER
THREE TIMES GOVERNOR
OF MINNESOTA

Johnson memorial. He did eventually produce one memorial figure for a Minnesota location and it was his last completed work as he died in an automobile accident shortly before the dedication of the "Thomas Lowry" monument in 1915. Lowry was neither a political figure nor a war

Minneapolis businessman "Thomas Lowry" (1915), seen
in this memorial by Karl Bitter, was involved with development of the streetcar lines in the Twin Cities. The
requirements of a differing form of transportation (the
construction of Interstate Highway 94) made it necessary
to move the monument from its original location in 1967.

hero, but rather a Minneapolis businessman financially interested in the city's streetcar company. When he died his family decided that a memorial was in order. The location would be a triangle of land in the midst of the Hennepin and Lyndale Avenue South intersection, where the monument remained until 1967, when it was moved south to another triangle of land bounded by Emerson Avenue, 24th Street, and Hennepin Avenue South. The bronze figure of Thomas Lowry wearing a morning coat and carrying his tall hat in his hand, stands in front of a tall granite screen which is pierced in two places. These breaks in the screen allow two seated figures (carved by Charles Wells) to be placed in the spaces. A sculptor toils on the left building the community while a woman picks grapes on the right echoing the carved words: "The lesson of a public-spirited life is as a tree ever bearing new fruit." Lowry stands at an angle to the viewer, an asymmetrical stance which art historian James Dennis says the sculptor often used (Dennis 1967: 192) and which makes its subject seem ready to welcome visitors to the city he had worked to create. Bitter never met Lowry, but he borrowed Lowry's clothing for verisimilitude. The clothes were modelled by a Bavarian grocer from St. Paul who was of the same approximate height and weight as Lowry.

In the early years of the twentieth century, before and for a while after the First World War, the ladies of the Daughters of the American Revolution were busy placing historical memorials in various places throughout the state. Markers, plaques on boulders and the Gateway Flagstaff were part of their program. In a Winona cemetery the grave of the only Revolutionary War veteran buried in Minnesota, Stephen Taylor, was enhanced with a small frontier fort built around it. Other D.A.R. chapters sponsored sculpture like the cast of Houdon's "George Washington" (1931) in Fair Oaks Park of Minneapolis, the statue of "Nathan Hale" (1907) by William Ordway Partridge on Summit Avenue, and the Celtic Cross (1923) at Shadow Falls, both in St. Paul.

When members of the Minneapolis monument chapter of the D.A.R. thought of a major patriotic memorial they selected a flagstaff. Not just a flagstaff one hundred feet tall, but a flagstaff which would have its own endowment for future maintenance. As Mrs. M. H. Coolidge, the chairman of the flagstaff committee said to a reporter as they were beginning the project:

> It is too far away to talk of other monuments, but it is the desire of every member of the chapter to give several patriotic monuments to the city. We want them to be practical, to teach a lesson, and we believe that all of the people of Minneapolis are with us in this effort. American cities do not have as many monuments as they should, and no city can have too many. The staff will add to the beauty of the Gateway park, and we believe it will always be prized as a municipal possession.
> (*Minneapolis Journal*, October 3, 1915.)

The committee raised funds through direct gifts, a bazaar, and a ball held at the Leamington Hotel. The flagstaff was designed by the architectural firm of Hewitt and Brown, and the bronze relief medallions and eagles are the work of John Karl Daniels. The flagstaff, dedicated on the Fourth of July in 1917, no longer shares the beauty of Gateway Park or Bridge Square since urban renewal has rearranged that entire part of downtown Minneapolis. The Gateway (now Phelps) fountain was moved to the Lake Harriet Rose Garden, the Gateway pavilion was demolished, and Daniels "Pioneers" sculpture banished to northeast Minneapolis. During the reconstruction the relief of Washington was stolen so the sculptor, then aged ninety-one, created a replacement for the flagstaff (*Minneapolis Star*, May 17, 1966). The D.A.R. flagstaff, minus the "city beautiful" surroundings of the Gateway, still holds its flag aloft at the intersection of First Street and Hennepin Avenue.

Anyone who tries to portray a popular hero, very recently dead, probably runs into the same sort of criticism that O'Connor did with his statue of Governor Johnson. "Everybody" as Jimmy Durante used to say, "wants to get into the act," and give their critical opinion. For Charles Brioschi, there would be no such problems with his statue of Christopher Columbus as no one really can be sure what the explorer looked like. In 1927 citizens of Italian descent organized a Columbus Memorial Association. Charles Brioschi was a member of that group and was asked to do the planned monument. Brioschi, born in Italy, had come to St. Paul with Adolfo Minuti in 1909 to open the city's first firm of architectural sculptors. They had worked with Stanford White and Cass Gilbert in New York and Washington, D. C. before moving west. Among their Minnesota projects were architectural sculptures for buildings at the University of Minnesota, the St. Paul Hotel, and the Minnesota Club (both in St. Paul), the court house in Milaca, and the Hibbing high school.

Charles Brioschi's "Christopher Columbus" was an overlifesize bronze, standing with maps in one hand on a granite base in front of a wall with benches. When it was dedicated on October 12, 1931, public schools in St. Paul were closed so students could march from Rice Park to the Capitol Mall for the event. The Columbus statue was erected through the efforts of a private committee just like those for the earlier statues of Wennerberg and Schiller. While citizens continued to form private committees to raise funds for monuments of heroes, governments at all levels (city, state and federal) entered the world of cultural support in the nineteen thirties. An overview of that public support for outdoor sculpture is the subject for a later chapter.

2   Monuments in Silent Cities

"A hilly area on the edge of town with well-maintained grass lawns, winding roads and a fence with tall gates" sounds like a city park. When this description is expanded to include "large and small marble or granite markers" then it is clear that a silent city or cemetery is being described. Most Minnesota towns set land aside for burials at the edge of residential and business developments. Hilly land, not suitable for building a house or factory, made for a good park as well as a picturesque town burial ground. Within the cemetery, plots were seldom fenced as that made upkeep difficult. As cemetery names such as "Oakland," "Oakwood," "Green Hill," or "Lakewood" suggest, trees were an integral part of cemetery design. Traditional flowers of grief such as roses and lilies were welcomed as funeral offerings although most cemeteries later posted signs explaining how long live flowers could remain before being discarded. Planners who designed parks were hired to plan the larger cemeteries, following the "rural cemetery" ideas of Andrew Jackson Downing. Horace W. S. Cleveland, an important landscape architect, designed Oakland cemetery in St. Paul, as well as Lakewood cemetery in Minneapolis.

Some cemetery areas were set aside for the burials of war veterans, firemen who died in the line of duty, the clergy, and members of lodges such as the Elks and Odd Fellows. A statue would be placed in such an area and then be surrounded by a small sea of grave markers, identical in size and shape. In St. Paul identical cast iron figures of firemen were chosen for the fire department's burial areas in the city's Catholic (Calvary)

Oakland and Calvary cemeteries in St. Paul were given identical cast iron figures of heroic firemen in 1901. Both statues stand on acanthus leaf capitals, grasping the handles of missing lanterns.

Eli Harvey's "Elk" (1906) honors members of the Elks lodges throughout the country. "Elks Rest" in Minneapolis' Lakewood cemetery received this guardian figure in 1917.

and Protestant (Oakland) cemeteries. This fireman figure carries a child he has rescued in his left arm and holds a lantern in his right hand. As the lanterns have often been stolen, the firemen now only carry lanterns when memorial services take place. A statue of a fireman in dress uniform can also be seen in Minneapolis' Lakewood cemetery. In Red Wing's Oakwood cemetery the fireman figure is dressed for work with boots and fire hose. All of these figures date between 1890 and 1900.

Figures of Civil War soldiers were placed in the areas set aside for burial of veterans, but sometimes patriotic groups preferred a single memorial for those who served in all wars. Near both the G.A.R. Soldier and the "Firefighter

Monument" in Lakewood cemetery is the "Soldier's Memorial," dedicated on May 26, 1923. This monument has three sections or pylons. On the top of the granite pylon honoring the Civil War veterans are a soldier's cap and belt of bronze. Flanking pylons to the left (Spanish-American War) and right (World War I) also carry bronze replicas of soldiers' equipment. On the right, the pile includes hat, belt, canteen, blanket and bayonet holder, while on the left are a helmet, cartridge belt, gas mask and canteen. A bronze eagle looks down on the entire composition of war memories and relics.

Animals occasionally appear as quite appropriate memorial symbols. Faithful lions, lambs and dogs can all be found on funeral monuments, but for Elks' Rest in Lakewood cemetery (where members of the Elks Lodge are buried) the lifesize bronze guardian figure of an elk, the work of animal sculptor Eli Harvey, stands on a rock. In St. Peter's Greenhill cemetery a small cement elephant stands above the graves of the Engesser family, who owned a local travelling circus.

Certainly most of the markers and monuments in any cemetery reflect private funding and personal taste, as well as what was locally available for purchase. Presumably many monuments were obtained through monument companies which, in turn, could obtain some mass-produced items, while other memorials were the work of stone masons or sculptors on their staffs. For private monuments the identities of sculptors are much harder to discover than they are for public monuments, for the latter are mentioned in newspaper accounts or in the records of monument committees. Funeral monuments do not always exemplify great sculpture. Laurence Schmeckebier wrote that "the sculpture of the cemetery, in this region, as in almost every other American community during the same period, represents without doubt its lowest form of artistic expression." This may have been, he felt, because the pioneers didn't like figural sculpture (Schmeckebier 1945: 17).

Fashion in the late nineteenth century called for numerous tall shafts or columns with sorrowful ladies on top. On other monuments of

Many of Lakewood cemetery's sad, walking ladies mourn atop tall columns. Nellie Walker's graceful figure dates from 1920.

The tree stump tomb is found in many older Minnesota cemeteries. Ivy and ferns climb its bark while the book of the dead set against the trunk is propped open to receive further entries. On this tree stump monument in St. Paul's Oakland cemetery a personal reference was added by the small locomotive seen at the base.

this era pensive, grieving women sit on lower bases, strew flower petals, or more actively mourn by clutching crosses. Derived from the walking, weeping ladies is Nellie V. Walker's bronze figure in Lakewood cemetery. Miss Walker was a student of Lorado Taft and received commissions for large memorials as well as more intimate studies of children.

Before 1931 statues and monuments carved in soft stone such as limestone were often commissioned. After that date because modern tools made it easier and cheaper to fashion headstones of harder stone with names and dates only, hand-carved and elaborate monuments became quite rare. The twenty-four foot tall figure called "Love" which was commissioned for the grave of Dr. Herman S. Dreschler in 1947 is therefore unusual. First, a copy of a statue in Milan, Italy had to be made. Then the copy and a young Italian stone carver, Giuseppi Omatti, came to Vermont and spent two years reproducing "Love" for St Paul's Calvary cemetery. The standing robed female figure steps down towards the viewer, offering a lily in one hand and carrying the remainder of her bouquet in the other. The pedestal is flanked by Ionic columns and a pair of urns stand on the lowest level, all carved of the same Vermont granite.

Perhaps one reason families are reluctant to purchase separate sculpture for funeral monuments is not the expense, but the sad possibility of vandalism or theft. A bronze, lifesize angel in Oakland cemetery is regularly defaced with spray paint and recently was knocked from its pedestal and broken. All of the small sculptures were recently stolen from another St. Paul cemetery.

Other religious funeral monuments feature saints, crucifixion scenes, or angels. Obelisks, draped or curtained urns, and rock cairns were

sometimes selected as appropriate funeral imagery, but the most fascinating of these memorials are the Tree Stump Tombs. These are not unique to Minnesota as Warren Roberts wrote a brief report on such tombs in Indiana (Roberts 1985). The basic design for these dead trees of life was a tree trunk with carefully delineated bark and branches reduced to protruding stumps. Ferns, lily fronds, and ivy climb up the trunk from ground level. The pages of an open book lean against the tree or against a barkless section, providing space for the names and dates of the deceased. Carvers told Roberts that the height of the trunk represented the length of the individual's life, and the branch stumps indicated children. Other details personalize the tree stump tombs: a railroad engine, boat anchors, a child's hat hanging on the trunk, and toys placed around the base. A ribboned hat and toys appear on the tomb of Andrew Humble (1852–1883) in St. Paul's Oakland cemetery. The tree stump is short and split as befits Mr. Humble's brief life.

Tree bark chairs are sometimes provided as adjuncts to a taller tomb or figures may stand with a small stump as a support or prop. Civil War soldier Henry Bagley (in the Udolpho cemetery north of Austin), a small boy named Willie Lee (in Stillwater's Fairview cemetery) and two very young girls in Minneapolis' Lakewood cemetery are all depicted with a short tree stump almost as if they had wandered onto a prepared stage and posed for their portraits in front of the stump. The sculptors who created the memorials for the two little girls, Lila George and Martha Neumuth, in Lakewood cemetery placed each child in front of a waist-high stump. Each child grasps the stump's one bit of branch in her right hand, while holding either a dove or flowers close to her chest with her left hand. Each child's hat lies on the ground at her feet. Both children were born in 1885 and died in 1891. A third, somewhat simpler monument, remembers Ella Louise Hankenson, who died in 1888 at the age of five years. All of these tree stump tombs were carved of limestone, range in height from twelve inches to twelve or more feet, and can be dated (on the basis of the earliest death dates noted) from the late 1870's to nearly 1910.

The figure of "Henry Bagley" (1906) in the Udolpho cemetery north of Austin was modelled from a photograph. The Union veteran stands in front of a short tree stump and holds a wreath of victory over his gun.

3 Remembering the Warriors

Minnesota made the transition from territory to state in 1858 just as America's struggle over slavery was intensifying. In 1861 Governor Alexander Ramsey was in Washington, D. C. on business when the attack on Fort Sumter took place. Ramsey immediately offered a thousand men for the country's defense. As William Watts Folwell wrote, "Without doubt Minnesota has the credit of making the first tender of troops for the great contest thus suddenly precipitated" (Folwell 1924: II, 77). When the news reached Minnesota via the new telegraph lines, men of the St. Paul Pioneer Guards volunteered for what was at first thought to be only three month's service, as that was the length of time then legally authorized for a call up of state militias. The first man to sign up in Saint Paul was Josias R. King (1832–1916). King served with the First Minnesota Infantry Regiment. Just as King was the first volunteer for the Union Army nationally, Albert Woolson (1847–1956) became the last survivor of the Civil War. Woolson served with the First Regiment Heavy Artillery, Minnesota Volunteers, and later was a national officer of the G.A.R. Figures of both King and Woolson can be found among Minnesota's small platoon of Civil War memorial statues.

The first memorial to Minnesota's veterans was erected on the battlefield of Gettysburg in 1867. It was a six foot high marble pedestal with an urn on top. On the pedestal were the words:

The dead shall not have died in vain.
All time is the milennium of their glory.
(Folwell 1924: II, 314.)

Survivors of the First Minnesota Infantry Regiment had sold their regimental band instruments to fund the monument. Thirty years later the State of Minesota allocated $20,000 for a more elaborate memorial (erected in 1897) with a charging soldier in bronze done by Jakob Fjelde to replace the simple urn (Folwell, *op. cit.* infra.)

After the War ended in 1865 annual encampments kept the battle memories alive for the Minnesota veterans. The first such meeting was held in St. Paul in 1866; the seventy-fifth and last took place in 1941, just a few months before yet another war erupted. The encampments united the men and the posts of the Grand Army of the Republic, the organization founded to look after veterans' needs. Making sure that the war service of their members was honored and the dead remembered were major goals for all G.A.R. posts. The importance of the memory was given poetic form by a local writer, Grace Craig Stork, in the Pipestone newspaper at the time. One verse of her poem, "The Veteran Speaks" read:

We tell you what we know
Beside these graves—the glorious long ago
Proud mem'ry holdeth last
Not even to bring back our vanished youth
would we give up that past . . .
(*Pipestone County Star*, May 24, 1901.)

Memorial Day at the end of May became the annual focal point for G.A.R. activities. The custom of decorating veteran's graves with flowers began in Columbus, Mississippi, in 1866. The idea quickly spread and Decoration Day, as it was first known, became a national holiday in 1868. Processions of veterans to the local cemetery, music played by marching bands, the offering of floral tributes, and patriotic speeches made by political leaders all were part of every Memorial Day. It became THE day to unveil a Soldier's Monument whether the veteran was uniformed for duty in the Civil War, in the South Pacific, or in Vietnam.

Most G.A.R. posts raised money for local outdoor memorials or even as the Frank Daggett Post No. 35 did in Litchfield, for a G.A.R. Hall (in 1885). The stereotype of soldier's memorials located on court house lawns remains, yet some were located in parks and cemeteries and some had no effigy figures at all. Some posts chose to list the names of those who had served on plaques set in boulders, markers, shafts or even benches, some perhaps with a bronze eagle on top. However, it is only the representational figures which have been included in this survey. Statewide there are more than two dozen Civil War memorials with figural forms. There are more Civil War monuments than those erected for any other war. Minnesota historian William Watts Folwell thought that was a great mistake. In a footnote describing the Civil War battle paintings which hang in the State Capitol building, he wrote:

> The author takes the occasion to express the opinion that such memorials of a war between sister states in the American Union are not in good taste. The Roman custom of preserving no memorials of a civil war is one that America, now united forever, may properly follow.
>
> (Folwell 1924: II, note 17, 327.)

Raising the money for a monument took time whether it was $500 for a white bronze soldier like Castle Rock's or the thousands of dollars needed for an effigy in granite or bronze. Often members of several G.A.R. posts pooled their efforts, with added contributions received from members of related organizations such as the Ladies of the G.A.R., the Women's Relief Corps, or the Sons or Daughters of Union Veterans. City or county governments and the state contributed dollars to monument funds and pennies were donated by local school children. Whether to place the soldier's monument in the city's park, or on the court house lawn, or even in the cemetery was sometimes a matter of debate, but in Carver County the problem was over which city should have the monument. Waconia's town council offered $813 to the fund. So today the grey bronze statue with a furled flag and only the hilt of his sword (the blade is missing) stands in Waconia's city park. Needless to say citizens of other Carver county communities may not have been pleased and, at the dedication of this memorial, Chaska people "were conspicuous by their absence." It was, according to one of the speakers, "the first monument erected to the memory of the veterans by county aid and public subscription." So, the article noted, "well done for Carver County" (Waconia, *Carver County News*, June 24, 1892).

Undoubtedly rivalry and civic pride were involved in the Civil War memorials. When Detroit (now, Detroit Lakes) dedicated its "Soldiers and Sailors Memorial" in 1915, the reporter carefully noted that shaft, figure, and base were all of Barre granite. A few paragraphs later he wrote, "The monument, it is said, is the only one in Northwestern Minnesota which has the marble statute (sic) surmounting the shaft. There are numerous ones which have a bronze statute (sic), but is generally admitted that these do not stand the elements and the effect of time as do those which are all of marble" (*The Detroit Record*, June 4, 1915). Both bronze and granite figures seem to have endured the weather quite well, but their guns and swords are often missing.

Although Civil War statues placed on extremely tall shafts were erected in eastern cities quite soon after the war, that was not the case in Minnesota. Most of the county memorials were dedicated years later and occasionally listed the names of Spanish American War veterans on the pedestals as well. In a typical case the John E. Rawlins post of Minneapolis spent more than a decade raising funds for the city's second Civil War Monument. A soldier's memorial had already been placed in Lakewood Cemetery in 1903, but for the G.A.R. circle on Victory Memorial Drive the goal was a statue of Abraham Lincoln. Fundraising began in 1916, stopped during the First World War, and began again after that war ended. When the granite for the base cracked during the carving the committee wrote to the granite company that some of the veterans were concerned that they might not live to see the dedication of the monument. This Lincoln statue, a composite effort, finally was unveiled on Memorial Day in 1930. According to F. Lauriston Bullard, the head is the work of Max Bachman while the body is a replica of Augustus Saint-Gaudens' standing Lincoln of 1887 (Bullard 1952: 282–283). In Chicago Saint-Gaudens had posed the president as if he had just risen from an armchair, but the $7500 raised in Minneapolis was not ample enough for a replica of the chair. All ten G.A.R. posts in the city eventually contributed, as did other groups, and $800 in pennies came from school children (*Minneapolis Journal*, November 24, 1929).

In St. Cloud twenty-six organizations con-

This bronze Civil War memorial was erected in Minneapolis' Lakewood cemetery in 1903 by members of local G.A.R. posts.

tributed to a Civil War memorial erected in 1918. All the donor names are listed on the pedestal in a patriotic roll call beginning with the Elks and ending with the Gustavus Adolphus Sick Benefit Society. Abraham Lincoln, holding a rolled Emancipation Proclamation in one hand, stands on this St. Cloud pedestal. The Memorial is now located next to an apartment building at 1st

"Abraham Lincoln" (1931) was placed on Victory Memorial Drive in Minneapolis to honor the city's Civil War veterans.

Street and 4th Avenue North. This Lincoln statue is one of eight based on an 1898 design by Alfonso Pelzer and was made of sheet copper by the William Mullins Company of Salem, Ohio. Pelzer's other Minnesota statue is the enormous "Hermann the Cheruscan" in New Ulm's Hermann Heights Park. Seven other Pelzer Lincolns were made and originally stood in Ohio, Idaho, New Jersey, Michigan, and Nebraska. The Mullins Company supplied the statue with a small base, leaving the pedestal size, with space for different inscriptions or donor lists, to the discretion of the monument committees.

Another Civil War figure produced by the Mullins Company can be seen in the Ortonville and Litchfield cemeteries. This soldier was fully equipped with bedroll on his back, and canteen and bayonet hanging from his belt. The figure could be furnished gilded, as Litchfield's was. The cost, according to Ortonville G.A.R. records, was $250 for the figure. Ortonville selected Cold Spring granite for the pedestal, which cost $255 more, but Litchfield chose whitewashed cement blocks to contrast with the shiny figure.

G.A.R. posts and veteran's families often obtained figures from local statuary or funeral monument companies. Thus, the same white bronze soldier figure dressed in overcoat, pants, cape thrown back over one shoulder, and with rifle placed at parade rest, was selected by G.A.R. posts in Spring Valley, White Bear Lake, Castle Rock and by the family of Samuel Bloomer. The stock design for a base featured arches, columns and symbols in relief, but Bloomer's pedestal is covered with text. The birth and death dates of his wife and children, details of his own life, and the major events of his war record are given on the four panels. Bloomer (1835–1917), color bearer for the First Minnesota Infantry regiment, took an active part in G.A.R. affairs. When Louis Muller Post No. 14 unveiled their monument on the lawn of the old Washington county court house at Pine and Fourth Streets in Stillwater in April of 1917, Bloomer was an honored guest. He died on the fourth of October of that year. The Stillwater monument which Bloomer helped to dedicate, showing a Civil War soldier ready for

Seven other examples of Alfonso Pelzer's "Abraham Lincoln" (1898) were made for eastern cities. St. Cloud's "Lincoln," fabricated in 1918, was funded by twenty-six patriotic and fraternal groups.

Spring Valley's "Civil War Memorial" (1892) includes the same soldier (standing at parade rest) seen in other Minnesota monuments, but each base is different. Spring Valley's soldier, who had lost his gun, was repaired in 1989.

battle, was the work of a Boston sculptor named Kohlhagen. It stands on a stone base which carries over 900 names of men from Stillwater and Washington county who served in the Civil War. Not all of the artists of Civil War monuments can be identified from either G.A.R. post records or newspaper accounts, yet some well known artists are noted. Pipestone's granite sculpture (dedicated in 1901) was the work of local artist and mayor Leon H. Moore; John Karl Daniels did the bronze figure of Josias King for St. Paul, while Duluth's two Civil War-related monuments were by Avard T. Fairbanks of Utah and Paul Wayland Bartlett. The Duluth "Soldiers and Sailors Memorial" (1919), located in front of the St. Louis County Court House, was designed by Cass Gilbert, but its seated "Patriotism Guards the Flag" figure in red granite is the work of Bartlett. In Canal Park the seated bronze of Albert Woolson shows him wearing his G.A.R. medal-covered jacket with his veteran's cap nearby. The sculpture was completed in 1955 when its subject, the last Union army survivor, was aged 108. The first cast of the Woolson statue was placed in the Gettysburg National Cemetery. The second cast, made in 1983, was given by the artist's family to the St. Louis County Historical Society. Members of the Veterans of Foreign Wars arranged to have it placed in Canal Park.

The Woolson and King statues are two of the four memorials which represent known in-

Stillwater's "Civil War Soldier" (1917) stands on a base listing hundreds of names of G.A.R. members from Washington county. The Perkins and Kratzert memorial is located in front of the old court house at West Pine and Fourth Streets.

Cass Gilbert designed Duluth's tall "Soldiers and Sailors Monument" (1919) for the plaza in front of City Hall. The red granite figure of "Patriotism" seated fiercely at the base of the flagpole is the work of Paul Wayland Bartlett.

Avard T. Fairbanks' sculpture of Albert Woolson, "The Last Survivor" (1955), was recast in 1983 as a gift to the city of Duluth. It now rests on a stainless steel base in Canal Park.

"Colonel William Colvill" (1909) commanded the First Minnesota Regiment at the battle of Gettysburg. He died in St. Paul on the eve of the dedication of the new state capitol building in 1905. Casts of Mrs. George Backus' bronze figure of the Colonel can be seen in the Capitol and at his grave site in the Cannon Falls cemetery.

dividuals. The other two are a limestone funeral monument in the Udolpho cemetery near Austin which was said to be an excellent likeness of veteran Henry Bagley (1845–1906), and the bronze statue of Colonel William S. Colvill (1830–1905) located in the Cannon Falls cemetery. Colvill enlisted in the Goodhue Volunteers and rose to become a colonel of the First Minnesota Infantry Regiment. Colvill and his men became instantly famous when they received orders to charge a much larger Confederate force at Gettysburg. Their bravery saved the Union Army, but their stunning losses were the greatest suffered by any Union regiment during the Civil War (Kunz 1958: 39). A Minneapolis sculptor, Mrs. George J. Backus, did a life size bronze statue of the Colonel for the Minnesota State Capitol. A replica was later placed at his grave in the Cannon Falls cemetery. Colvill is shown in uniform, wearing a slouch hat and grasping an officer's sabre in his right hand.

Two other memorials to prominent Minnesota men have a Civil War connection. In the center of the University of St. Thomas in St. Paul, an institution of higher learning which he founded, is a bronze statue of Archbishop John Ireland (1839–1918). Michael Price's statue celebrates the Archbishop's work as an educator and priest, but his service as a Civil War chaplain was equally well known. John Karl Daniels' bronze monument to Governor Knute Nelson (1843–1923) also places other figures around the pedestal on which the chunky Governor stands. Nelson, a Norwegian immigrant, came to America as a child. His Civil War service was with a Wisconsin regiment, and he moved to Minnesota after the war. His immigrant and military backgrounds are emphasized in the figures flanking the pedestal.

Memorials to battles and individuals involved in the Sioux Uprising of 1862 are mainly located in the area of southwestern Minnesota where this conflict took place. Most of the monuments are of the tall shaft variety, and honor the settlers rather than their Indian opponents. Sculpture which focuses on the Sioux experience also exists, but is far more recent in nature. In

Hutchinson two statues of Little Crow (1818–1863), the Sioux leader, have stood on the same stone base next to the Crow River. The first, in cement, was the work of famed wildlife artist Les Kouba, a native of Hutchinson. That figure was on view from 1937 to 1982, when it was replaced by a bronze figure designed by Kouba and modelled by Robert Johnson. Little Crow was killed near Hutchinson in 1863. The forty Sioux hung at Mankato are remembered by name in a series of metal signs created by Edgar Hachivi Heap of Birds. The signs (called "Building Minnesota") were commissioned by the Walker Art Center as part of the Cheyenne sculptor's one man show in 1990. Later they were to be placed in a Mankato park. "Winter Warrior" (1987), a statue carved in Kasota limestone by Thomas Miller, sits on a pedestal next to the Minnesota Valley Regional Library which now occupies the site of the mass execution.

Only one Minnesota statue was erected to remember those who served in the Spanish-American War, although lists of names of those veterans appear on memorials for other wars. Bearing the cheerful nickname of "The Hiker", this bronze figure was placed in front of the Armory on the University of Minnesota East Bank campus in 1906. "The Hiker" is the best known work of a Boston sculptor, Theo Alice Ruggles-Kitson. This figure has been reproduced fifty times for memorials ranging from New England south to Washington, D. C., and west to Michigan, Illinois and Minnesota. Mrs. Ruggles-Kitson became a specialist in military sculpture as she received commissions for numerous Civil War battlefield monuments in addition to her figure of "The Hiker."

The lawn in front of the Todd County Court House in Long Prairie is the site for a World War

The statue of "Archbishop John Ireland" (1989), educator, priest and Civil War chaplain, stands in the heart of the University of St. Thomas campus. On the pedestal sculptor Michael Price used relief panels of birds to symbolize various aspects of the Archbishop's life.

I monument which apparently was Minnesota's first. It was designed by state architect Clarence Johnson, and has a relief of a doughboy facing a wreath-carrying Victory figure on its north side. The relief carving is the work of John Karl Daniels. Side panels carry the lists of veterans' names from both the First and Second World Wars. Another relief which includes a First World War soldier can be seen above the entrance to the Willmar Memorial Auditorium. This auditorium, designed in 1935 by William Ingemann, was a WPA project. Three concrete panels over the entrance are the work of Samuel Sabean, a WPA sculptor whose other architectural relief work can be seen on the Milaca Town Hall and on the Minnesota State Fair Poultry and Horse Barns. A fully realized statue of a soldier cannot be found among Minnesota's First World War memorials. Only the thin shadows of low relief serve to recall the "War to End all Wars." Even the age-old image of the obelisk has been replaced by interlaces in architect Thomas Holyoke's granite Celtic Cross which stands in Shadow Falls park where St. Paul's Summit Avenue ends above the Mississippi River. Holyoke's First World War memorial was given to the city by members of the St. Paul chapter of the D.A.R. in 1923.

There may be two reasons for the lack of soldier effigy figures in memorials for World War I. One is clearly a matter of timing. As many Civil

State architect Clarence Johnston designed Todd County's "World War I Monument" (1920). The bronze relief of the soldier and Victory is the work of John Karl Daniels. The monument is located in front of the county court house in Long Prairie.

War monuments were erected fifty years after that conflict had ended, lists of veterans' names for the subsequent wars were simply added to Civil War memorial pedestals. There was also a national campaign to upgrade the war memorial. As the chairman, Charles Moore of the Metropolitan Museum of Art, wrote in an issue of the *American Magazine of Art* devoted to the subject:

Public art is the reflex and the index of public taste. If we have had bad art it is because we have bad taste. Certainly it is not because we do not spend enough money to get good things. No other people spend so much on 'art' as we spend. The trouble is that we get thistles for grapes and stones for bread (Moore 1919: 234).

In the same issue other writers noted what they felt were aesthetically successful war memorials and suggested other alternatives. Tablets, arches, fountains, and forests could all be planned and named in honor of war veterans. Above all the committee did not want to see more mass produced soldier figures. Representing Minnesota on the committee was John Van Derlip, a trustee of the Minneapolis Society of Fine Arts.

Minnesotans did follow this advice by dedicating groves of trees, auditoriums (such as Willmar's) and football stadiums (such as the University of Minnesota's) to the veterans. Honoring the veterans became one of the purposes of the newer patriotic groups, the Veterans of Foreign Wars (organized in 1902) and the American Legion (organized in 1919).

The following decades, during which World War II, Korea and Vietnam all summoned men and women to military service, are still perhaps too recent to support an outpouring of memorial art. War may frequently incite sculpture, but as the Civil War experience suggests, it requires time. Future memorials to these wars will prob-ably take the more abstract form of walls with names trying to capture the emotional impact of Maya Lin's "Vietnam Veterans Memorial Wall" in Washington, D. C. In downtown Red Wing, such a memorial to the veterans of all wars was dedicated by Minnesota's General John Vessey, Jr., the Army Chief of Staff, on May 21, 1988. The 351 veterans from Goodhue County are listed on six separate granite markers, one for each war, arranged in a circle around a flagpole. Several blocks away, looking down from its site on the court house lawn, is Red Wing's earlier Civil War Memorial, dedicated in 1913.

Mankato has two war memorials, both the work of Thomas Miller, whose "Winter Warrior" was mentioned previously. In Wheeler Park is Miller's Second World War Memorial in Kasota stone which incorporates the "Ruptured Duck" discharge emblem. His "Blue Earth and Nicollet Counties Vietnam Memorial" (1988) is located south of the city on Stoltzman Road. The focal point is a granite boulder from which a rippling flag emerges. Around the flag boulder are the service dates and names of the veterans, each lettered on an oversize replica of a soldier's identification name plate or "dog tag."

Several memorials in St. Paul deal with the Vietnam War. Paul Granlund's "Man-Nam" bronze of 1970, located on the grounds of the Governor's Residence, focuses in shape and palindromic name on the positive and negative aspects of that conflict. "Man-Nam", one of Granlund's earliest public sculptures, was commissioned through a competition organized by Iantha Levander, the then governor's wife.

The Capitol Mall, the land sloping down from the front steps of the Minnesota State Capitol Building to the Veteran's Admninistration Building, seems increasingly to be the favored site

Vietnam veterans from Blue Earth and Nicollet counties were honored in this "War Memorial" (1988) off Stoltzman Road in Mankato. The flag supporting boulder and surrounding dog tags are the work of Thomas Miller.

The ruptured duck symbol of World War II was carved on top of this war memorial (1989) in North Mankato's Wheeler Park. Under the wing of the duck can be seen the signature of artist Thomas Meagher Miller.

for memorial sculpture. West of the Veteran's Administation Building is Rodger Brodin's "Monument to the Living — Why Do You Forget Me?" (1982), a twelve foot high soldier made of welded steel. Brodin, a veteran of the Vietnam War, who has specialized in sculpture involving military and police subjects, also did a bronze group for a small plaza in front of the Veteran's Administration Medical Center in Minneapolis. In this figural group, "The Price of Freedom is Visible Here" (1987) a medical corpsman leads his wounded buddy to a nurse. Brodin's most recent sculpture is one of Minnesota's few Second World War memorials. This ten foot bronze honors Marine private Richard Keith Sorenson (born in 1924) from Anoka, who received the Medal of Honor for gallantry during the battle of Namur Island, Kwajalein Atoll in the Marshall Islands in 1944. Sorenson was present at the dedication of the figure at the Veteran's Memorial site, opposite John Ward Park in Anoka, on Memorial Day, 1991.

As yet uncompleted is a State memorial to the Vietnam war, to be built on the Capitol Mall. A team of sculptors (Stanton Sears, Jake Castillo and Nina Ackerman) won a competition for the memorial with an entry entitled "Lake Front D. M. Z." Components of their project involve a wall with names, markers for hometowns, walkways, and trees and pools to emphasize that war's geographic experience as Minnesotans came in lengthy contact with Southeast Asia.

Minnesotans, both men and women, served in the Persian Gulf campaign of 1991. The veterans of Desert Storm were welcomed home with parades and at least one monument to an earlier war was decorated with Desert Storm's ubiquitous symbol. The granite Civil War soldier in front of the Lyon County Court House in Mar-

shall still stands at eternal attention, but in the summer of 1991 he could be seen clutching a yellow ribbon above his rifle.

When celebrations honoring the conclusion of the Persian Gulf war were held in Marshall, the Civil War soldier (1911) in front of the Lyon County Court House was ready. Rather than a laurel wreath of victory, he held a big yellow ribbon on his gun.

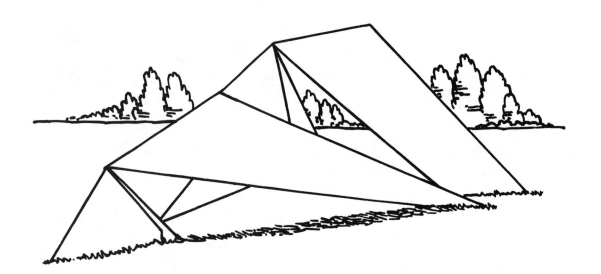

4 Public Art Programs from the Thirties On

The alphabet soup of federal and state art programs began in the 1930's. Like everybody else during the Depression, artists lacked jobs so the first program, PWAP (Public Works of Art Program), was set up to help them. As painter Syd Fossum described the experience in a column written for the *Minneapolis Star,* the director of the Minneapolis Institute of Arts, Russell Plimpton, chose the artists in Section Ten (the PWAP's designation for Minnesota, Wisconsin and Illinois). Most came from the Twin Cities and each had a production quota. For a weekly salary of $28.50 or $42.50 each artist was expected to produce a set number of watercolors, oil paintings, sculptures or prints. A Technical Committee of artists then evaluated the work which was supposed to reflect "the American scene." All of the art accepted could then be allocated to state institutions (Fossum 1966). Before the PWAP ended exhibits of the art were completed. For Section Ten the exhibit was held at the Minneapolis Institute of Arts in March, 1934; a survey of work from the entire country was held at the Corcoran Gallery in Washington, D. C. from April through May of 1934. The PWAP lasted from December, 1933 until June, 1934 when, it was hoped, the relief assistance would no longer be needed. Sculptors included on the PWAP list were John Karl Daniels, Otto Dallmann, and Samuel Sabean.

Next came the FERA (Federal Emergency Relief Act), a short-lived program which funded art classes in the Sexton Building in Minneapolis with artists hired as teachers. The director, sculptor Charles Wells, was very proud that the FERA classes, offered to anybody over sixteen and out of school, were free (*Minneapolis Journal,* January 20, 1935). Later, under the WPA, art classes continued to be offered at community art centers in Duluth, in St. Paul (at the old Post Office building at Fifth and Market Streets) and at the Walker Art Center in Minneapolis.

The most famous of these art centers was certainly the Walker, which began as an exhibition space for T. B. Walker's private art collection. In January, 1939 the Minnesota Arts Council was given control of the collection and galleries and asked to raise money so that a community art center could be established. Daniel S. Defenbacher was hired as the new director (Johnson 1976: 9–12). Walker's art school was directed by Mac LeSueur from 1940 until 1950, and its teacher of sculpture was Evelyn Raymond.

Two other programs, the Treasury Section of Painting and Sculpture (1934–1938), and the Treasury Relief Art Project (TRAP) from 1935–1939 were managed by the Treasury Department. Under both programs contracts were awarded to artists for the decoration of federal buildings such as post offices and courthouses. The goal was to find quality professional art for governmental buildings. The Treasury Section used funds set aside by Congress in the construction budget for new federal buildings which, in this case, was one percent of the final cost. This program included murals and sculpture for the Justice and Post Office buildings in Washington, D. C. Later on the Section (renamed the Section of Fine Arts) conducted competitions for post offices nationwide, for the Interior and War Department and Social Security buildings, and for the government building at the New York World's Fair (O'Connor 1969: 21–25). One of the Section's most famous mural competitions was one to provide a mural for a designated post office in each state. The "Forty-Eight State Competition" is thoroughly analyzed in Karal Ann Marling's *Wall-to-Wall America* (1982). TRAP hired artists from the relief lists to provide paintings or sculpture for existing federal buildings (O'Connor 1969: 25–26).

The longest lasting and best known of the art programs was the WPA/FAP (Works Progress Administration/ Federal Art Project) which began in 1935 and was terminated in June of 1943. In Minnesota this program was directed by painter Clement Haupers until he was promoted to serve as an assistant to the National Director of the WPA/FAP, Holger Cahill. Samuel Sabean directed the sculpture section from 1935 to 1938.

Finding a list of all sculpture produced under the auspices of the depression programs in Minnesota is difficult. Francis O'Connor presented a table giving totals of art works produced under the various programs in his *Federal Support for the Visual Arts: The New Deal and Now* (1969). O'Connor listed totals for murals, easel paintings (which included watercolors), sculpture and prints. Under sculpture he gave the following totals for the entire country:

PWAP:	647
Section of Fine Arts:	301
WPA/FAP:	17,744
TRAP:	65.

(O'Connor 1969: 54.)

What O'Connor listed is not defined as to location (outdoors or inside) or type (architectural or free standing), although the many small craft figures were probably not included. For comparison, the number of works completed by Minnesota sculptors during the PWAP period totalled six: two freestanding figures, three bas-reliefs and one bust (*PWAP Files*, Minnesota Historical Society Archives).

What has been termed "pedestal" sculpture was allocated to state institutions and lists, especially of the many small items, are hard to find. Larger works and relief or architectural sculpture exist but are not always clearly identified. A "Final Report" for the Minnesota WPA/FAP (ca. 1940) listed the colleges, schools, and hospitals where sculpture had been sent. This report noted that wood carving had been done for four locations and that twelve schools had received sets of Chaucer's Canterbury Tales figures. Two sculptures were "in progress": one for Little Falls and the "Leonidas Merritt" statue for Mountain Iron. The Merritt statue and some of the Canterbury Tales figures were the work of Robert Crump. Another list, published in the *American Art Annual*, lists sculpture by two artists completed under WPA auspices. Alonzo Hauser created reliefs for the Park Rapids postoffice and Brenda Putnam completed interior sculpture work for the St. Cloud postoffice (now demolished).

Obviously under these programs sculpture was not widely produced, nor is it, even today, widely documented. Samuel Sabean produced the relief panels on the Willmar War Memorial Auditorium, a relief panel over the entrance to the former town hall (now the library) at Milaca, reliefs on buildings at the Minnesota State Fairgrounds, and a fountain figure for Chisholm High School. Alonzo Hauser's relief figures still hang on a wall inside the Park Rapids postoffice. Evelyn Raymond did a large concrete relief for the International Falls High School stadium and two smaller wood panels which hang in a hallway in the Sebeka High School opposite a large mural by Richard Haines.

Miss Raymond's experience with her International Falls bas relief seemed to fulfill several program aims of the WPA. She was asked to work on the molds in the lobby of the Walker Art Center so that the public could watch an artist at work. This plan continued until the molds became so heavy that the museum staff began to worry about the strength of the floor, so artist and molds were moved to the basement. When the molds were complete Miss Raymond and a crew of WPA assistants went to International Falls to pour the concrete at the site. Pouring concrete in the "Icebox of the Nation" in January was a test of skill and endurance but the artist recalls the camaraderie of the experience with pleasure. Her relief of football players can still be seen above the entrance to the high school stadium.

Two sculptures in the round were the result of WPA funding and both are located in Minnesota Iron Range communities. In Mountain Iron a ten foot six inch portrait figure of Leonidas Merritt (1844–1926) looks down from the grounds of the public library. In front of the Merritt statue is a nine and one half ton granite boulder known as the "Rock" which symbolizes the ore Merritt and his brothers found. The figure was molded of a mixture of granite chips and cement by Robert Crump. Merritt is shown as the timber cruiser he was when he first discovered iron ore and his pack is firmly attached to his back.

The Willmar War Memorial Auditorium (1935–1936), designed by William Ingemann, was placed on the National Register of Historic Sites in 1991. Three relief panels over its entrance doors were the work of Samuel Sabean. The central panel shows the figure of Peace standing between the soldier and sailor.

The bronze sculpture of Frank Hibbing (1856–1897) stands in a fenced enclosure in that city's park. The bronze, by Hibbing artist Robert Mitchell, shows the man who platted the townsite and then opened its first sawmill, bank, waterplant, and electric light system.

Of the three sculptors mentioned, only Evelyn Raymond continued to play an important role in Minnesota art circles after the WPA experience. Miss Raymond taught sculpture at Walker Art Center from 1941 through 1953. She has exhibited widely and received numerous commissions for sculpture in stone or hammered copper. Her double figure called "Legacy" stands in the courtyard of Minneapolis' Fairview Hospital and her portrait figure of Maria Sanford represents Minnesota in the National Hall of Statuary in the United States Capitol. For her the WPA was not only a job, but an opportunity to learn techniques from other sculptors and to share her abilities as a teacher.

Unconnected with any federal program yet paid for by the federal government was the "Chippewa Brave" statue by Carl C. Mose. This serene looking bronze stands in the clearing on the north bank of the Red Lake River near the village of Huot. Here in 1863 chiefs of the Pembina and Red Lake bands signed the Old Crossing Treaty with Alexander Ramsey representing

One of the few freestanding outdoor sculptures to be completed under WPA auspices is this figure of "Leonidas Merritt" (1940). Artist Robert Crump shows Merritt as a timber cruiser; his pack is on his back, a hammer in one hand, and ore sample in the other. The figure stands on the grounds of the Mountain Iron library.

the United States. By this treaty Chippewa land became open to white settlement and agricultural development. Carl Mose, a Danish-born sculptor, taught at the Minneapolis School of Art and at Carleton College, and later worked in the Washington, D. C. area.

Both Minneapolis and St. Paul commissioned major civic sculptures in the 1930's, projects which were not linked to any of the various federal and state art programs. For Minneapolis, the work was "Pioneers," a massive carved granite block from which summit a family of figures emerges. An old man and a young family represented the settling of the city while in relief on the base Father Hennepin discovers the Falls of St. Anthony. This work, by John Karl Daniels, was placed in 1936 in front of the city postoffice on Marquette Avenue between 1st and 2nd Streets in what was then called Pioneer Square. In 1965 the city offered the sculpture to anyone who was willing to remove it from the path of urban renewal. What the city and park board had once paid $20,000 for suddenly had no value. In 1967 "Pioneers" was moved to a triangular plot of land at Marshall Avenue and North East Main Street, where it can be found today.

Naturally the predicament faced by his "Pioneers" sculpture was greatly upsetting to the artist who was then ninety years old. Daniels had one of the longest careers of any Minnesota sculptor. The statue of Josias King (1903) was probably his earliest outdoor commission, and

A bronze statue of "Frank Hibbing" was placed in Hibbing Park in 1941. Local artist Robert Mitchell portrayed the town's original planner dressed as a miner.

Ojibwe leaders met with representatives of the federal government to sign the Old Crossing treaty in this wooded glade in 1863. Carl Mose's bronze pipe-bearing figure, "Chippewa Brave" (1933), stands at the site on the banks of the Red Lake river near the village of Huot.

one of several war memorials which he did. In a heroic vein he created a governor (Knute Nelson) at the State Capitol, a founding father (George Washington) at Austin, and two versions of explorer Leif Erikson for St. Paul and Duluth. His work exists in bronze, stone and glazed terra cotta, carved, cast or modeled in relief. Early on in his career he demonstrated butter sculpture at the Minnesota State Fair (Marling 1987: 226–227) and quite late in life he carved the red granite buffalo which looms from the terrace of the North American Life Insurance Company building on Hennepin Avenue in Minneapolis. Daniels studied with Andrew O'Connor in Paris, but spent most of his career in the Twin Cities.

In St. Paul a new city hall and courthouse for Ramsey County was built in 1930–1931. Relief decoration over and flanking its entrances was designed by Lee Lawrie, best known for his work on the Nebraska State Capitol Building. The sleek dark interior concourse leads to the dramatically lit and revolving "God of Peace" by Carl Milles. This thirty-six foot tall Indian figure, nicknamed "Onyx John," functions as both a town symbol (Garvey 1981) and a war memorial of a type which the war memorial committee of 1919 would certainly have approved.

Another Minnesota governor died in office in 1936 and his portrait statue was Charles Brioschi's last major work. As Floyd B. Olson (1896–1936), the state's first Farmer-Labor party governor, came from north Minneapolis the plans at one time had been for a large development in his honor containing a stadium, a park and his boyhood home restored as a museum. In the end only a statue was realized, but it exists in two places. The first statue stands on a tall pedestal along the renamed Olson Memorial Highway in Minneapolis. Brioschi, his son Amerigo, and Louis Kirchner created this work. In 1958 Amerigo Brioschi was asked to recreate the Olson statue for a location on the Capitol Mall to the west of the "John A. Johnson" memorial. This time Olson stands in front of a low wall as if to balance the Columbus figure with its low wall at the east end of the upper mall.

The public art programs of the thirties are often cited as the forerunners, the impetus, and the catalyst for all later public art programs. Programs of the 1930's provided jobs for artists who taught and produced art, and through competition or direct commission provided art for public buildings. The PWAP, FERA, TRAP and WPA/FAP, however were limited in duration either by legal design or by the advent of World War II. The art programs begun subsequently also provided jobs, commissions, grants and subsidies, but despite funding cuts and program changes, they seem to be more solidly entrenched in government bureaucracy after twenty-five years. Governmental support for both the performing and visual arts, despite criticism over what they

Judge Henry Weber asked sculptor John Karl Daniels to reproduce his favorite image of the first president in this statue of "George Washington" (1937) for the children of Austin. The figure is located on the lawn of the Mower County Court House.

John Karl Daniels' granite "Buffalo" (1948) was commissioned as a corporate symbol for a life insurance company located on Hennepin Avenue. It has become one of Minneapolis' best known outdoor sculptures.

fund, how much they support and what is seen as censorship, have come to be accepted as an appropriate use of public resources.

Establishment of the two national endowments (one for the arts and one for the humanities, known as NEA and NEH) in 1965 was followed by the founding of the Minnesota State Arts Council, later to be changed to "Board" (MSAB). Minnesota is divided into eleven regional councils, each of which oversees programs and allocations of money in its area. Guidelines for some regional councils forbid any grants for murals or sculpture while other areas permit such support, often co-sponsored by foundations and other groups. In fact, the need for raising locally such "matching funds" is virtually a universal requirement for many of these programs. The need to raise matching funds has led to the more active participation of private and corporate foundations such as the Bush, Jerome, Northwest Area, Dayton-Hudson, and McKnight, in arts development in Minnesota.

In 1981 a ten year listing of NEA-funded projects was published (Beardsley, 1981). Eleven Minnesota grants were listed for that decade; including two temporary installations and a five state tour by a circus. Of the sculpture projects noted, George Morrison's "Feather Motif" and Jackie Ferrara's "A 193 Epistyle" in Minneapolis and David von Schlegell's "The Gate" at a rest stop near Duluth can still be seen, but Robert Irwin's project for the University of Minnesota ended at the discussion stage.

One of the temporary installations, called "9 Artists/9 Spaces" endured memorable problems. The police confiscated one art work (a billboard featuring a prone Foshay Tower) thinking it was a bomb, another work was so vandalized that it needed to be relocated, a brush pile on a wooden platform was removed from the Capitol Mall as a potential fire hazard, and a neon light display was removed from a black neighborhood after criticism that it was "irrelevant to the black community" (Steele, 1971). An editorial titled "The Art the Public Couldn't See" commented that "many people in the Twin Cities are the poorer for being deprived of the chance to view several unique, provocative works of sculpture. Like them or not, approve or disapprove, we believe that most people would have preferred to judge these works for themselves" (*Minneapolis Tribune*, September 5, 1970).

Destruction of a temporary sculpture exhibit and attacks by vandals on permanent outdoor art works have continued since that time, as other examples indicate. Whether stealing the bow from Ole Bull's violin or the umbrella from columnist Barbara Flanagan's sidewalk cafe table are only malicious pranks rather than acts of deliberate disapproval is hard to say. The gang member eager to spray his name or symbol on any object within his group's perceived turf wrecks just as much damage to the outdoor sculpture as does the thief or aesthetic censor. What this means in times of economic problems for the preservation of artworks is that a stolen bust (like that of "Henrik Ibsen" in Como Park) or the bow of a Norwegian violinist may not be replaced and that vandalized artworks which could cost too much to repair are simply removed from view.

Like the Treasury Section of Fine Arts program of the 1930's, the Art-in-Architecture Program of the General Service Administration (1963-to date) provided art for newly built federal buildings. In the beginning this was a program supported by presidential policy rather than by law. Thus it could be and was suspended from time to time (Thalacker 1980: xxi.) The cost of any artwork was to be no more than one half of one percent of the construction budget although that percentage could also change. The process of choosing art and artist, however, has been unchanged since 1973. As described by Donald Thalacker, the architect suggests where art might be placed and what type of art should be commissioned. The GSA then asks the NEA to select a panel of art professionals (at least one of whom must be from the geographic area where the project will be built) to nominate three to five artists for the commission. The GSA Administrator then reviews the panel's nominations and selects the artist to receive the actual commission.

Between 1972 and 1979 only one work was commissioned for a federal building in Minnesota and, as Thalacker wrote, the project "seemed jinxed from the very beginning" (Thalacker 1980: 149). In 1965 Haarstick Lundgren & Associates, the architects for the Federal Courthouse in St. Paul, suggested that an outdoor sculpture would be appropriate art for their project. The Art-in-Architecture program had been suspended at that time so it was not until 1973 that a panel (composed of Martin Friedman, director of the Walker Art Center; Paul Smith, dean of Hamline University; Dean Myhr, executive director of the State Arts Board; and architect Louis Lundgren) was appointed. A year later sculptor Charles Ginnever was notified that he had received the commission. Then came more probems as the artist wanted his contract to include a permanent maintenance clause as well as a resale royalty provision which the GSA would not sign. The agency was having trouble at the same time finding money to finance the project so it was not until 1976 that the contract was finally signed and the maquette for the sculpture approved. When Gin-

never's "Protagoras" was installed later that year local approval was not universal. The parallelograms of Cor-ten steel were described as a "nasty accident" by Ozzie St. George in the *St. Paul Pioneer Press* (May 25, 1976). In St. George's account a flat bed trailer had obviously misjudged the corner of Robert Street and Kellogg Boulevard and left the pile of steel in a heap as a result. Sandblasted Cor-ten steel is intended to weather and rust over the years, but Wisconsin's Senator William Proxmire gave GSA one of his "Golden Fleece of the Month" awards for wasting the taxpayer's money and, as an example, cited "Protagoras" which he considered "a rusty piece of farm machinery left out in the field" (Thalacker 1980: 151).

Similar criticism was leveled at other art works made of large scale industrial steel which were erected in Mankato and South St. Paul, but although these sculptures were located on public property, they were funded with private money so the question of "taxpayer" dollars couldn't be raised. Dale Eldred's "Mankato Piece" (1968) used trusses from an old railroad bridge while Philip Ogle chose I-beams of Cor-ten steel for his kinetic sculpture attached to a masonry retaining wall along South Concord Street in South St. Paul. Eldred's metal "x" shapes first marked a spot at South Second and Hickory Streets, but because of building construction had to be moved in 1981 to the north end of the Pike Street parking ramp. When "Mankato Piece" was unveiled in 1968, editor Ken E. Berg of the *Mankato Free Press* quoted sculptor Eldred's belief that "a sculpture should represent the celebration of man and his environment, not technology" (*Mankato Free Press*, June 19, 1968). Thirteen years later another Berg column noted that "Mankato Piece" had now become a part of the city's heritage, although what it was supposed to represent was unclear. In fact, concluded Berg, "That's one nice thing about identifying with the 'Mankato Piece'—everybody's conclusion about its message is correct" (*Mankato Free Press,* June 8, 1981). Ogle's work also drew some perplexed comment when first installed, but, like the Eldred work, it continues to be part of Minnesota's outdoor art collection.

Two other city projects were recipients of state arts board grants which then had to be matched by funds raised locally. Both works were done by Minnesota sculptors and had local links in subject matter and material. For the "Granite City" of St. Cloud, Anthony Caponi designed "The Granite Trio," three huge rock forms which stand outside the downtown Mall St. Germain. Despite their size and solidity, "The Granite Trio's" boulders are user-friendly. Relief detail contrasts with their bulk while handholds make it clear they can be touched and climbed.

Steve Jaenisch, a sculptor from Fergus Falls, was asked by the town of Tracy to create a work in memory of one of their most devastating experiences, the tornado of 1968. His "Tornado Tree" (1990) reproduced in steel rods the shape of an elm tree which was bent and stripped of its bark by the fury of that storm, yet survived for another twenty-two years. The tornado killed nine people and destroyed many homes in this small southwestern Minnesota community. Jaenisch's "Tornado Tree" stands in a small park along Highway 14 as a symbol of that event (*Tracy Headlight-Herald,* June 6, 1990).

In the 1970's community art programs using CETA (Comprehensive Employment Training Act) funds were able to hire artists. In Minneapolis, sculptors working in the City Art Productions program produced a series of small totem poles which once stood outside a building at 3045 Park Avenue South, but are now missing. A temporary exhibit near Minnehaha Creek in 1978 included works by Jack Becker, Mark Heffelfinger, Rich Cooper and Sean McLaughlin. Heffelfinger's stainless steel "Ashoka" is now located at the Minnetonka Arts Center. Becker went on to found Forecast, a nonprofit alternative arts organization in 1978. Forecast, artist-directed and artist-run, has exhibited everything from traditional forms of painting and sculpture to films, videos, performance art, dance and experimental work. For the first year Forecast had its own gallery space at 416 First Avenue in the warehouse district of Minneapolis. Since then, Forecast's exhibits have been indoors and out, throughout the Twin Cities. Two exhibits, "Indigenous Minnesota Sculpture" (1985) and "Art of the Eye" (1986) received Twin Cities Mayor's Public Art awards.

In St. Paul, COMPAS (Community Programs in the Arts and Sciences) was allocated its first CETA positions in 1976. Among these first seven "ArtsPeople" was one sculptor, Steve Beyer. Two works by Beyer, in St. Paul's Douglas Park and at the St. Paul-Ramsey Arts and Science Center park, were done during his COMPAS days. Most of COMPAS's artists worked on neighborhood murals (documented in MUSEUM OF THE STREETS: Minnesota's Contemporary Outdoor Murals. Pogo Press: 1987), taught classes in arts and crafts, or worked with theater and puppetry troupes. Residencies by artists and poets spread COMPAS' activities across the state from its base in St. Paul. In the most recent furor over possible cuts in NEA programs, Garrison Keillor testified before a Congressional committee on his experience as a COMPAS writer in residence and the importance of that experience to

In 1978 Mark Heffelfinger's stainless steel "Ashoka" was shown in a Minneapolis City Arts exhibit in Minnehaha park. Photograph courtesy of Mary Degen.

his future career (*The New York Times*, April 14, 1990).

The city Arts Commission of Minneapolis, founded in 1974, has launched several new programs to make art available to more of the city's residents. Through its Art in Public Places program open competitions were held to select artists to design manhole covers and bus stop benches. The eleven cast brass manhole covers, set in the sidewalks near the downtown City Center development, were designed by Marcia Stone and Wes Janz, Keith A. Leaman, David Atkinson, Karen Hansen, Stuart D. Klipper, Wayne Salzman, Robert Corbet, Craig Smith, Juris Curiskis, Craig L. Main, and Frank Antoncich. Designing manhole covers, measuring twenty-one and three quarters inches in diameter, proved a very popular task as 460 designs were entered in the competition. The manhole covers were dedicated in 1984 and received an award from CUE (the Committee on Urban Environment).

In 1987 the Arts Commission selected four winners in a second competition for art in downtown Minneapolis. The four selected were Leslie Hawk, Thomas Rose, Stanton Sears and Bryan Carpenter. Their four benches are quite different in style and theme. Thomas Rose's "Chippendale Couch" is set outside the Minneapolis Public Library, suggesting that patrons might read on its overstuffed bronze seat while they wait for the bus. Leslie Hawk's brightly colored "Oasis" features llamas, a pelican, a monkey, and palm trees offering a colorful spot to wait for a bus. Stanton Sears called his bronze air mattress "Minneapolis Water Toy Bench." His bench seems to float over fish, a wave and an overturned boat. Sears later used similar motifs for his "Siscowet Bench" whose air mattress is supported by fish,

an anchor, a wave, and a net with tiny fish. The "Siscowet Bench," a project of the Duluth Arts Commission and the Minnesota State Arts Board, is located near Lake Superior in the Bayfront Festival Park.

The farthest south of the benches, Bryan Carpenter's "Bus Top Bench," emerged from the sidewalk near the Minneapolis Community College. Carpenter's sheet metal bus top in regulation MTC red suggested a bus emerging from a tunnel towards waiting passengers. Passengers and passersby didn't wait patiently or treat the bus benches very respectfully. All of the bus-stop benches were along busy Hennepin Avenue. Vandalism made removal and repair of the benches necessary within two years. After conservation work all but Carpenter's bus bench went back to their original locations. His was moved to a new and presumably safer spot at Thomas Avenue and West Lake Street.

An additional bench project, called "All the World's a Stage," was commissioned by the Arts Commission with funds from the *Minneapolis Star Tribune*. For this tribute to long time newspaper columnist Barbara Flanagan, artists Bruce Wright and Mark Nichols placed five wirebacked chairs around a small table with its own umbrella. Ms. Flanagan, who had often written in praise of sidewalk cafes, could have her own table where she could sit with coffee and notebook, surrounded by emblems of some of her journalistic campaigns: a carousel horse and a trumpet for the Lake Harriet Bandshell. The umbrella was later stolen so at present the entire Barbara Flanagan installation is in storage awaiting repair.

The benches are part of the Arts Commission's Art in Public Places Program which in 1989 commissioned a bronze statue of Hubert H. Humphrey (1911–1978) by Rodger Brodin. The

Humphrey statue now stands at the south entrance to City Hall, recalling the beginning of Humphrey's political career as mayor of Minneapolis.

"Tranquility Rise" (1989), another project funded through the Art in Public Places Program, has several different elements located in North Commons Park of Minneapolis. Designed by artist Seitu Jones and built with the help of students from North High School, it included a stage with bench seating and cutout figures, a sitting area with benches and weathervane-topped poles, and a series of ceramic tiles set in a path connecting the stage and the hilltop sitting area. Some of the tiles were broken, others were stolen, and the structure on top of the hill was set on fire as it apparently had been built on what a local gang regarded as their turf.

Duluth established its Public Arts Commission in 1986. One of the Commission's responsibilities is implementation of this city's Community Arts set-aside ordinance. Under this ordinance any funding of five thousand dollars or more would have one percent of the construction costs set aside for the purchase of art works. Art can be obtained by commission or by purchase of existing work. Preference is given to artists who live in Duluth. Between 1987 and 1989 the Arts in Public Places program obtained fifteen items including Stanton Sears "Siscowet Bench." Since then a fountain by Ben Effington and a series of works along Canal Park Drive have been installed or are planned.

Another Minneapolis Arts Commission program, Minority Ethnic and Neighborhood Arts New Presenters Program, began in 1985 to fund a variety of other arts opportunities. A mural in the Harrison neighborhood, a Pow-Wow at Stewart park, dance classes and Hispanic music

and dance workshops are among its programs. A project proposal for a small park at 32nd Street and Chicago Avenue in Minneapolis was funded under this program. Sheryl McRoberts worked with students from Folwell Junior High School on the components for "Artstop" (1991). The small park now boasts a totem pole which carries terra cotta masks rather than carved wooden images, and plantings and a trellis guarded by one of the turtles from the annual May Day parade at Powderhorn Park.

Many of these recent public art projects emphasize community involvement in theme and location of art works. Neighborhood groups are encouraged to submit proposals for projects which would suit the needs of their residents and might be undertaken with participation by community members, a program which Minneapolis calls "Neighborhood Gateways."

Another project funded under the Minority Ethnic and Neighborhood Arts program included literal gateways in its design. Each of the wooden arches was painted with motifs the young artists had selected to represent their own ethnic backgrounds. Well concealed at its dedication on November 9, 1991, were the trees and bushes which should help to make the corner at 12th Avenue and Lake Street a place of beauty and a "Neighborhood Safe Art Spot" in more clement weather. The project's three directors, Marilyn Lindstrom, Baron Lewis and Walter Griffin worked with eleven teenagers to realize the project.

In 1988 the Minnesota legislature established a matching grant program for community improvements and clean-up. The idea was to spruce up the entire state before the United States Olympic Festival, scheduled for July, 1990, had taken place at venues throughout the Twin

A "Celebrate Minnesota 1990" grant helped Faribault citizens sponsor the "Bea Duncan Memorial Fountain" (1991) in their city's Heritage Park. In the bronze figures by Ivan Whillock trader Alexander Faribault can be seen examining a fur pelt offered by a Wapakuta Sioux hunter.

Cities. "Celebrate Minnesota 1990" was directed by the state Department of Trade and Economic Development. Communities were invited to develop local improvement projects, submit them to "Celebrate Minnesota," and then, if funded, the community would need to match the grant money with cash or in-kind contributions on a three to one ratio. Each town was required to purchase two highway signs from the Department of Transportation identifying their status as "Celebrate Minnesota 1990" communities. A third sign, made locally, was to be placed at the site of the funded project. Although most of the 182 communities did ask for money to clean up, restore, rebuild and erect highway signs, some grants were approved for public sculpture. These included Belgrade's huge Centennial Memorial with its fiberglass crow; the Rattvik horse in Cambridge; chainsaw sculpture in Embarrass; a bronze sculpture of a lumberman (based on the artist's grandfather) for Webber Park in Camden, by Rodger Brodin; and the "Bea Duncan Memorial Fountain" in Faribault by Ivan Whillock.

Mrs. Duncan, a teacher, was interested in local history, so two figures from Faribault's past stand on the fountain named for her in Heritage Square. Taopi, a Sioux leader, inspects a fur pelt held by fur trader Alexander Faribault on the fountain's pedestal. In commissioning their figures Camden and Cambridge added to existing parks, Belgrade and Embarrass built something new, and Faribault redeveloped space adjacent to its old railway depot. Other community grants funded moving "The World's Largest Snowman" to a more visible location on Highway 36 in North St. Paul and repairs to the pedestal of Eagle Bend's "Eagle." The base had begun to lean and as Eagle Bend's proposal noted, "each year it slowly leans a little more and we frequently hear from people passing through that they worry about our Eagle taking a dive" (*Celebrate Minnesota Archives*, Minnesota Department of Trade and Economic Development). All these communities thus followed the "Celebrate Minnesota" guidelines directed at cleaning up, stressing local heritage, and giving both residents and visitors new causes for local pride.

Those towns which have passed the century mark often celebrate with art. Town committees raise money for centennial murals or sculpture. Peter Quirt's "Eagle" for Eagle Bend and George Bassett's "The Harvest" for Winthrop are such century-markers. Bassett, who lives and works on his farm near Winnebago, has created a number of bronzes for southern Minnesota towns. In addition to Winthrop, his couple known as "The Delavan Pioneers" stands in a small park in Delavan, "The Danish Immigrant" was created for Lincoln Park in the Danish sec-

tion of Albert Lea, and "The Girl by the Pool" stands in Putnam Park of Blue Earth.

Another program which has a statewide impact is the Percent for Art in Public Places Program, begun in 1983. For any state building which costs over $500,000, an appropriation of no more than one percent can be made for the acquisition of art. Primary authority for the Percent of Art Program was given to the Department of Administration with actual management being delegated as of 1987 to the Minnesota State Arts Board. New construction could involve any sort of state building, even at a rest area or travel information office. South of Worthington on Highway 60 Janet Lofquist's "Habitat" (1989) can be seen in a field near the Travel and Information Center. The bronze boat-shaped form with its ribs of Cor-ten steel suggests prehistoric relics left undisturbed amid prairie grasses. Kinji Akagawa's "Four Seasons with a Sundial" (1984–1986) is a forest structure located at the Baptism River rest area in Tettegouche State Park on Highway 61 on the north shore of Lake Superior. Wood benches are set near boulders and bronze sundials in a design which changes feeling with the time of year.

When the Minnesota Historical Society decided to leave its original but cramped headquarters, Percent for Art projects were immediately possible: one at the new headquarters building under construction and the other at the old building which was transformed into the Minnesota Judicial Center. Space to the north of the old building has already been filled with Richard Fleischner's benches, walls and simple columns. At the new location the Percent for Art budget was shared by Brit Bunkley's etched glass panels, James Casebere's brass charms inlaid in the terrazzo floor, and Andrew Leicester's "Watergarden," located outside. Leicester's original concept for the new History Center's courtyard proved too expensive so the artist was asked to develop a new concept which would remain within the Percent for Art budget (*Minnesota Historical Society News,* September-October and November-December, 1991).

Many of the Percent for Art projects, however, have been on college campuses. The community colleges are the most recent additions to Minnesota's menu of higher education choices and new campuses need new buildings. Naturally not all Percent for Art projects fund outdoor sculpture. Painters, printmakers, sculptors, photographers, fibre and craft artists can all submit resumes and slides to be placed in the MSAB artist's registry. When a new construction project is announced a site selection committee is established which will decide what type of art, how to obtain it (direct purchase or commission), and whether to select the artist through open invitation or direct competition.

A short tour to see Percent for Art Projects would lead to Bemidji State University ("Crosswater" by Janet Lofquist), Faribault Technical College ("44 North" by Stuart Nielsen), Northland Community College at Thief River Falls ("Falls Thief" by Stanton Sears), and Normandale Community College in Bloomington (for an untitled work by Chuck Huntington). "St. Cloud Slapshot" by Cork Marcheschi and "Perspectives" by Chuck Huntington are recent additions to St. Cloud State University's collection of outdoor art, as Barry Tinsley's "Elliptical Trisect" was to the campus of the University of Minnesota at Duluth.

Minnesota's college campuses have always had art on display, sometimes the gifts of alumni or faculty, and sometimes the legacy, so-to-speak, of an artist in residence. By far the longest residency has been that of Paul T. Granlund at Gustavus Adolphus College at St. Peter. Granlund had previously taught at the Minneapolis School of Art before moving to St. Peter in 1971. His work is located all over the campus, from the doors of the Chapel to the entrances of numerous buildings. Many students have had the opportunity to watch a Granlund work develop from model to finished casting in bronze at his Gustavus studio. As the Listing of Outdoor Sculpture reveals, Granlund's commissioned works appear in many other locations, ranging from churches to hospitals and banks. Granlund favors bronze for his circles of touching figures, often seen emerging from cubes which retain impressions of their forms.

St. Olaf College in Northfield recently acquired a very large collection of works by Kaare Nygaard, a Norwegian born dentist who turned to sculpture late in life. The Nygaard collection will eventually be placed throughout that hilly campus. Carleton College, also in Northfield, has several works by long-time faculty member Raymond Jacobson, and a huge multi-layered stone arch by Dimitri Hadzi. The University of Minnesota's outdoor art collection began early with the figures of "John Pillsbury" (1900) by Daniel Chester French and "The Hiker" (1906) by Theo Alice Ruggles-Kitson. On a terrace above the un-

derground Williamson Hall is Stewart Luckman's gleaming tubular stainless steel "Rokker V" (1981). This statue was commissioned by the University's Alumni Association to commemorate its seventy-fifth anniversary. Melvin Waldfogel, director of the University Gallery, organized an exhibition called "Process" to explain the development of this project and the production of the sculpture. Such information, he wrote in the catalogue introduction, is not always retained (*Process*, 1981).

One of Paul Granlund's largest and longest bronzes stands near the Administration building at St. Olaf College in Northfield. There are four components to "Celebration" (1982), each based on a variant of a tetrahedron. The figures imprinted on this side of the "Community" section suggest a dance of life.

On the University's West Bank campus are Alexander Liberman's "Prometheus" attached to the north wall of Blegen Hall, John Rood's "Don Quixote" next to the law school, and Siah Armajani's garden of sculptural amenities in front of the Hubert Humphrey Institute. At the University's horticultural facility in Chanhassen, the Minnesota Landscape Arboretum, more sculpture is set near ponds and gardens, in hosta glades, herb gardens, and in the crabapple orchards. Works by Katherine Nash, Chuck Huntington, Andrew Leicester and Paul Granlund can be seen there. In Duluth the Tweed Art Museum of the University of Minnesota has a sculpture garden with Lipchitz's "Sieur Duluth."

Since World War II the list of professional sculptors who have taught at Minnesota's colleges and universities is a long one. Alonzo Haus-er, Anthony Caponi, and Stanton Sears at Macalester College; John Rood, Evelyn Raymond, Katherine Nash and Thomas Rose at the University of Minnesota; Paul Granlund, Charles Wells, Kinji Akagawa, and Michael Bigger at the Minneapolis College of Art and Design (formerly the Minneapolis School of Art); Raymond Jacobson at Carleton College; Stewart Luckman at Bethel College; Michael Price and Cliff Garten at Hamline University; Norman Holen at Augsburg College; and Peter Lupori at the College of St. Catherine, are but a few of the names which should be mentioned. Most of these men and women continue to exhibit their work and accept commissions as public artists, following the double path of artist and teacher which began in the 1930's in classes such as those at the Sexton Building.

Stewart Luckman's "Rokker V" (1981) commemorates the seventy-fifth
anniversary of the University of Minnesota Alumni Association. The tubular
stainless steel work was placed beside Williamson Hall on the University's east
bank campus. Photograph courtesy of the artist.

5 All the World's Biggest—a Flock of Town Symbols

A town symbol represents pride in a community, in its natural or geographic situation, and in its mythic or actual past. Town symbols stand in gathering places for civic events and celebrations, marking the land with benches set nearby for people and spaces for cars. The most successful town symbols embody the town's persona; they represent the town in the greater world so that when somebody sees the "Little Mermaid," for instance, he thinks immediately of Copenhagen, or perhaps of Albert Lea.

Minnesota has many town symbols, large and small, proclaiming the virtues (and senses of humor) of its towns, large and small. Many have been planned and financed by local chambers of commerce to advertise those communities, area hunting or fishing opportunities, and local summer or winter festivals. What better way to stress hunting or fishing than by building a very, very, large walleye, deer, or trout? And for towns named Moose Lake, Blackduck, Pelican Rapids, or Eagle Bend, the spirit of place seems to call for visual form in concrete, fiberglass or even copper. The history of these town symbols can be traced by the materials used. The Age of Concrete is followed by the Age of Fiberglass which

is now being supplemented by the Age of Wood carved by the chainsaw.

When the statue is finished, with its park arranged around it, then postcards and promotional literature will be used to carry its image far and wide.

Around town the town symbol may be difficult to ignore. It's up there, painted on the watertower, or flapping on the banners hanging from the lightpoles along Main Street. Some town symbols serve as mascots for the high school sport teams so they are equally hard to escape at games, homecoming events or reunions. And then there are the parades.

Most Minnesota towns have annual celebrations. Parades for the Fourth of July, harvest festivals, and winter sports contests all mark civic calendars. Seasonal listings published by the state's Department of Tourism in its quarterly publication, *Explorer*, note hundreds of events. Town symbols are featured every time. A portable symbol rides on a float with the festival princess and often that unit represents the town at other festivals in the region.

When Garrison bought its fiberglass "Walleye" from Creative Displays in Sparta, Wiscon-

Canada geese are found at virtually every urban lake and park, but only Fergus Falls boasts of an almost airborne sculpture of a giant goose. Steve Jaenisch's "Goose" (1990) is made of welded steel rods and can be seen above the lawn of the Otter Tail Historical Society.

sin, the giant fish was built on supports which could be placed on a flatbed trailer so Miss Garrison and her faithful fish could ride the float in style. Preston's fiberglass "Trout" rests permanently on its float in a small park on Highway 52, welcoming visitors and awaiting future Junes with future Trout Days. In 1983 when the Madison Chamber of Commerce acquired its twenty-five foot long codfish, columnist Jim Klobuchar quoted Dick Jackson of Madison on Lou T. Fisk:

As far as I know, this is the biggest codfish in America. It's just as big as the Jolly Green Giant that sticks up over the freeway outside of Le Sueur, only we're horizontal. It's not only big but portable. This is a codfish that deserves an audience, so we're making it adaptable to parades. You've got a parade, we'll come with the codfish.
(*Minneapolis Star Tribune*, April 26, 1983.)

Unlike other Minnesota fish sculptures, Madison's cod stands far from any waterside, but the image of "Lou T. Fisk" appears on banners, the watertower, and in a brand new chainsaw carving. "Lou T. Fisk" no longer travels, but in 1987, the cod was sent on a goodwill tour to all other towns named Madison. While it may sound as if only fiberglass fish swim the parade routes the custom was never so restricted. Lindstrom's "Karl Oskar and Kristina," the Emigrant couple, were parade regulars for years in the summer festival named for them before finally retiring to a pedestal in front of the Chisago County Press office. "Big Ole" the Viking from Alexandria, spent the summer of 1965 in New York at the World's Fair, but even before fiberglass made giant travelling figures possible, "Babe the Blue Ox" and the "Black Duck" were on the road.

Minnesota's most famous town symbols, "Paul Bunyan" and "Babe the Blue Ox" of Bemidji, not only started the fashion for giant statues in the state, but launched it in a parade. That is, Babe did. Paul was well sunk into the ground on the shore of Lake Bemidji. Paul has never moved. Babe was constructed of wood, wire and canvas at the county highway department and did manage to ride, mounted on a Model T. Both figures were built for Bemidji's first *Paul Bunyan Winter Carnival*, held from January 14–17, 1937. Car caravans and trains brought visitors to the carnival events and Babe was sent to greet them. The friendly blue ox then led visitors on a tour of downtown although his tin horns had to be turned or removed completely so they wouldn't

Even fiberglass statues need refurbishing every so often. In the summer of 1991 it was time for cosmetic repairs to "Big Ole the Viking" (1965). Gordon Shumaker's figure stands proud and tall in the heart of downtown Alexandria.

snag the street decorations (*Bemidji Daily Pioneer*, January 13, 1937). Babe was such a success in parades that crowds saw him at the St. Paul Winter Carnival, the Minnesota State Fair, the Thief River Falls Corn Festival, and other events that year. Press coverage of Paul and Babe was widespread, including *Life* Magazine and the *New York Times*. Attendance for the Carnival itself was estimated to be 15,000 for the first year and 100,000 people in 1938 (*Bemidji Daily Pioneer*, January 17, 1937 and January 18, 1938).

The following year the small town of Blackduck, 25 miles northeast of Bemidji, decided to participate in Paul Bunyan's carnival. After all, Paul had certainly hunted in their neighborhood, so their entry could show his target. Leaders in the local Civic and Commerce Association set to work to design a float, a black duck, and a rifle for Paul. Many town symbols evolved this way. One person suggests the idea, the civic group helps raise money for supplies, and a committee builds it.

The "Black Duck" was built at Camp Rabideau, the local Civilian Conservation Corps (CCC) camp, under the direction of P. J. St. Amant, the forest ranger. The float had huge

At first "Babe the Blue Ox" (1937) was made of wood and wire. His horns were tin and removable; his eyes were automobile tail lights. This 1937 Hakkerup real photo postcard shows how he appeared in Bemidji's Winter Carnival parades.

Babe, Paul's Blue Ox
Hak
Bemidji, Minn.

When Blackduck's "Black Duck" (1938) wasn't riding in parades he rested in front of the town creamery. The fence shown in this Hakkerup real photo postcard is gone and the "Black Duck" now is flanked by Paul Bunyan's own blunderbuss.

sleigh runners and room for the duck, the wooden rifle, and the Blackduck queen (Virginia Sullivan), who wore a white satin figure skating costume trimmed with black fur and a black accordion pleated cape. Blackduck's float preceded "Babe the Blue Ox" in the Bemidji parade and they made a noisy couple. Paul's blunderbuss fired and a hose connected to the exhaust pipe under Babe allowed the ox to snort clouds of smoke (*Bemidji Daily Pioneer*, January 15, 1938).

Visitors from the Twin Cities were quick to invite the "Black Duck" south. He spent one week in a Dayton's display window (the glass had to be removed to insert the sixteen foot duck from the sidewalk) and he rode in the 1938 St. Paul Winter Carnival parade. A Blackduck reporter commented sadly that the duck's size also caused trouble in St. Paul:

Considerable difficulty had been experienced by the Blackduck group in making arrangements and in getting the huge float out of the auditorium basement where it had to be assembled. They found the doors were not made wide enough for Paul Bunyan's huge relics and had to be satisfied with bringing up the rear of the parade instead of the coveted position in the first division which had been awarded by parade officials. This was due mainly because the duck was too high to leave the auditorium by the exit provided and had to be turned around and driven back through the main entrance after making the official entry to the auditorium. (*Blackduck American*, February 2, 1938.)

A story in a St. Paul newspaper noted that the Black Duck, if real, would be enough for 1,862¼ dinners (*St. Paul Pioneer Press*, January 30, 1938).

Concrete was the favored medium for Paul, Babe (after his parade days were over) and other early town symbols because it was relatively easy to use and cheap, even in the large quantity needed. The local committee would build the framework, someone would do the plastering, and somebody else would bring the creation to life with paint. Most of the outdoor figures need to be repainted every few years, but sometimes the repairs needed are more extensive, as is the case with the tall young lady of Hackensack. "Lucette Diana Kensack", the sweetheart of Paul Bunyan, was the brainchild of Doad Schroeder, a local grocery store owner. He designed "Lucette," built the framework with a trapdoor in her skirt for repairs, and gave "Lucette" her original paint job. The figure wears a solid color blouse, striped skirt, and holds her hands demurely in front of her. She stands on the shore of Birch Lake, facing the town. In 1991 the whims of weather were very cruel to "Lucette." First high winds blew her head off. A new head was then carved and painted by Jerry Faber, a woodcarver from Walker. Then a hailstorm severely damaged her hands and stripped away part of her back, exposing the board framework. As of September, 1991 that destruction had not been repaired, but according to local reports, plans were being made to do so as "Lucette" will mark a sprightly fortieth year in 1992.

"Lucette" is part of the second generation of Paul Bunyan figures, those erected from the 1950's on. Paul and Babe in Bemidji and their friendly black duck nearby began the story in the late thirties. The winter festivals continued but the idea of actively stimulating tourism in these northern Minnesota towns had to wait until the Second World War had ended. In 1949 Sherman Levis and Ray Kuehmichel purchased a "Paul Bunyan" figure built for an exhibit in Chicago by the Chicago and Northwestern Railroad and brought it home to Brainerd. Their "Paul Bunyan" is mechanized, is able to talk, and functions admirably as a tourist attraction rather than as a town symbol. (Brainerd's lightpole banners, in fact, feature the town's historic water tower rather than Paul Bunyan.) The Brainerd "Paul Bunyan" was placed in a log shelter. Other figures (such as "Sport the Reversible Dog" and "Henry the Giant Squirrel") occupy a courtyard picnic space in front of him. Around Paul's courtyard are carnival rides, a mini golf course, outdoor pool, and other attractions. The center is a summer attraction only, usually closed soon after Labor Day. Paul's faithful friend, however, can be seen at any time as this fiberglass "Babe" stands in the parking lot outside the entrance.

The largest of all the Bunyan figures is Akeley's, built in 1984–5 by various members of the Krotzer family. This Paul kneels, holding an axe in one hand with his other hand outstretched so those who wish can balance in it as they pose for photographs. This thirty-three foot high figure is made of fiberglass, a much more common choice of material by the 1980's, than the concrete used in Bemidji, Hackensack or Nevis.

West of the Bunyan heartland are more town symbols in concrete. Pelican Rapids' "Pelican" (1957) and Vergas' "Loon" (1963) were town projects, with those adept at framing, plastering, or painting each contributing appropriate labor. The twenty foot tall "Loon" oversees the beach at Long Lake while the fifteen and one half foot "Pelican" guards Mill Pond dam on the Pelican River, within the city limits.

Wheaton's "Mallard" (1960–1961) was the work of a high school art teacher and principal, Robert Bruns. He not only became interested in studying outdoor sculpture but added his own notable construction to the corpus. Information is not always available on the origins of any town symbol's design although "Lucette's" costume and capped hairstyle do suggest Walt Disney's Snow White. In an interview Bruns commented that his "Mallard" was based on "a paperweight duck, a Grain Belt Beer ad, and a dime-store statue" (Coleman, 1982).

According to a story written when "The Big Pelican" of Pelican Rapids was twenty-five years old, the source for its design was an actual bird which died of injuries and had been stuffed. Ted and Anton Resset, local metalworkers, made scale drawings of the stuffed bird and then fashioned a cardboard model to determine how tall to make both the figure and its base. The pelican figure had a steel framework covered with wire netting which was then plastered and painted. The pelican builders considered covering the bird with fiberglass, but rejected that material since they thought plaster would make it look more realistic. The "Pelican" has proven to be quite durable. As Truman Strand, chairman of the original committee, said at the pelican's birthday party in 1982, "If anyone damaged the Pelican, the whole town would be down on them . . . It's a part of all of us, no matter how long we've lived here" (*Pelican Rapids Press*, July 15, 1982).

The latest of the community concrete figures is Rothsay's "Booming Prairie Chicken," a Bicentennial project in 1976. Art Fosse designed the big bird; the park where it stands on Highway 94 is now named in his honor. A plaque at the park states that the thirteen foot tall sculpture was erected "to alert area visitors and remind local residents of the beauty to be found on the native prairie grasslands." No superheroes, no legends, just a large bird to help people remember a time when the land was full of prairie chickens, not houses or highways.

For any outdoor sculpture from the early heroes and soldiers to the town symbols, a dedication ceremony is vital. Certain days, like Memorial Day, or the town's annual festival become the right time for the event, but if the statue is not done or the speaker can't attend, committees learn to be flexible. When the Nevis Civic and Commerce Association decided to build the world's largest "Tiger Muskie" they wanted to invite a suitably famous person for the dedication and waited patiently until the Governor could come. The thirty foot six inch fish was done early in August, 1950, but the ceremony took place on August 23rd. Two thousand people attended and Governor Luther Youngdahl's speech was thought to be excellent since he talked about fishing, told Swedish jokes, "and refrained from politics entirely" (*Park Rapids Enterprise*, August 31, 1950). Since then the annual *Muskie Days* have been held in July. The giant muskie has been repainted from time to time and now has a wooden roof for protection from the elements.

Fiberglass, the next material to find favor with town symbol committees, was invented in the 1930's. During the war years military applications for this extremely durable material took

Ever since "Smokey the Bear" (1954) appeared on posters and as a stuffed toy, he has been enormously popular. Gordon Shumaker's fiberglass figure in International Falls is probably the country's tallest firefighting bruin at a height of twenty-six feet.

precedence over all civilian uses. After World War II was over, boat builders began using it as a protective coating for wood and display makers discovered its commercial applications. Fiberglass was soon a favored material for outdoor signs and three dimensional billboards.

Fiberglass figures can be made in molds or, if they are of heroic size or larger, a metal armature is made and fiberglass is applied to sections which are then bolted together.

Two of the earliest fiberglass figures, "Smokey the Bear" (1954) in International Falls and the "Territorial Pioneer" (1959) at the Minnesota State Fair were made in Gordon Shumaker's workshop in Minneapolis. Shumaker had been designing floats for both the Aquatennial and Winter Carnival parades for years so he was accustomed to taking small commercial emblems (such as the Hamm's beer Bear) and enlarging them to float dimensions. Smokey, he once noted, had to be an absolutely accurate copy of the Forest Service bear so representatives of that agency came to Minnesota to make sure that it was. Among Shumaker's other well-known fiberglass figures are the State Fair "Gopher," the White Bear Lake "Polar Bear" (who graces an automobile dealership on Highway 61), and the giant "Bluegill" at Orr.

Robert Ed, a commercial artist whose training in sculpture began in Evelyn Raymond's classes, designed and built the Crane Lake "Voyageur" (1958) of fiberglass. The cheerful woodsman stands in a small park at the intersection of Highways 24 and 424, west of the town of Crane Lake. Over the years additional tablets and markers honoring local residents have been placed near the "Voyageur," creating a shrine of local history.

On the "Voyageur's" paddle a small metal tag bears the words "Sculptured Advertising." This company was founded by Robert Johnson and Ver Young, and operated in Minneapolis until Young moved to Sparta, Wisconsin. While not all of its fiberglass figures were purchased as town symbols, some have taken on that role later in life.

Among Johnson's own fiberglass figures are the fetching thirty foot "Mermaid" (1967) who beckons from the roof of the Mermaid Supper Club in Moundsview; the bright green revolving "Octopus" (1967) who dangles his sponges and other tools in front of a chain of car washes; the Minnesota Federal Savings and Loan Association "Eagle" (1958), and the Bank of Willmar's "Indian" (1956). The golden "Eagle" served as Minnesota Federal's logo at Fifth and Minnesota Streets in St. Paul until the logo was replaced in 1987. The association sought a new home for its eagle and Northwestern College in Roseville accepted the gift with pleasure. Perched on a rock the eagle, now the college's mascot, greets visitors at the college entrance.

The Willmar "Indian" has a somewhat more complex history, but, like the "Eagle," because

Robert Ed designed and built the "Crane Lake Voyageur" (1958). The fiberglass figure has now been joined by other markers honoring latter day local "voyageurs."

of a logo change it too made the transition from the world of commerce to symbol. The first Indian figure was created by Eben E. Lawson as a symbol for the Kandiyohi County Bank in 1915. That first small figure was broken, but a replacement figure served as a model when the bank, then renamed the Bank of Willmar, decided to have something larger made. Johnson's fiberglass figure, "Chief Kandiyohi," measured seventeen feet and stood over the bank entrance at Fifth and Litchfield Streets for the next twenty-seven years. As "Kandiyohi" is supposed to mean "abounding in buffalo fish" the figure carries fish in one hand and his trusty spear in the other. In 1983 the bank became the First American Bank and the longtime logo was immediately expendable. But, like the "Eagle," there was a new and presumably permanent home for the Indian. "Chief Kandiyohi" was accepted by the Kandiyohi County Board of Commissioners. The new location was a tall pedestal in front of the county court house. At the dedication of plaques explaining the statue's significance one speaker observed that the Indian figure now appeared on all county stationery and on some county vehicles. Another speaker commented that the statue "could mean as much to Willmar as the onyx Indian in St. Paul or Paul Bunyan in Bemidji" (*West Central Tribune* (Willmar), October 10, 1985).

The Sculptured Advertising firm changed

The gilded figure of "Chief Kandiyohi" (1956) spent many years standing above the entrance to a Willmar bank. In 1983 Robert Johnson's fiberglass figure was moved to a pedestal next to the Kandiyohi County Court House.

hands once more, gaining the name of Creative Displays in the process. Jerome Vettrus who had worked for that firm opened a new company called F.A.S.T. (Fiberglass Animals, Shapes, and Trademarks) with partner Norb Anderson in Sparta, Wisconsin in 1982. F.A.S.T. continues to market some of the Creative Displays molds, but has developed many new animals, fish, fountains and amusement park creatures. Visitors to Sparta have only to head north on Highway 21 keeping a sharp eye open for a giant hamburger or a buffalo on the left. F.A.S.T.'s dun-colored molds share land around the plant with its fully painted figures, offering a wondrous mix of animal, vegetable, and myth on the back forty.

Among Creative Displays' Minnesota figures are the "Jolly Green Giant" in Blue Earth (1978); the Crosby "Serpent" (1977); the Cloquet "Voyageur" (1976) and "Dala Horse" (1978); "Chief Wenonga" in Battle Lake (1979); "Chief Red Robe" in Thief River Falls (1976); Deerwood's "Leaping Stag" (1978); Aitkin's "Iron Worker" (1981); and "Robin Hood" (1982) in Sherwood Forest, north of Garrison.

Two of Creative Displays' Indian figures, one Chippewa and the other Sioux, stand outside of the Thunderbird Motel in Bloomington. Directly in front of the motel entrance is a fiberglass "Chief Thunderbird" by Robert Johnson. "Chief Thunderbird" seems to be the only equestrian figure in the state.

Bearing the F.A.S.T. label are Moose Lake's "Moose" (1989); Hill City's "Bear" (1985); the "Hobo" in Starbuck (1987); Preston's "Trout" (1988); Blackduck's newest "Black Duck" (1985); a standing "Chicken" in Delano (1990); the Remer "Eagle" (1983) and the great "Crow" of Belgrade (1990).

The largest collection of fiberglass figures

F.A.S.T. Corporation's giant fiberglass "Crow" (1990) is but one part of Belgrade's "Centennial Memorial." The eighteen foot bird, designed by Jerry Vettrus, welcomes visitors to "Crow Country" from its perch on top of a small walk-in museum.

anywhere in Minnesota is only a seasonal happening. In fact some friends of fiberglass have been known to observe that "spring has come since the animals are back at the State Fair Mini-Golf Course." F.A.S.T. co-owner Norb Anderson usually has eighteen of his firm's figures arranged as obstacles on the mini golf links on Como Avenue.

All of the fiberglass figures have some type of pedestal base or portable supports, but Belgrade's giant "Crow" has the tallest pedestal and most elaborate park of all. Guidelines for "Celebrate Minnesota" had suggested that towns seek ways to celebrate their history and welcome former residents home. Belgrade's eighteen foot "Crow" stands in a nest of branches atop a small museum located inside the pedestal. A large memorial wall made of over 4,000 individually purchased and inscribed bricks serves as a backdrop. Outside the wall's perimeter are cement picnic tables, each flying the flag of a different foreign country. Those whose ancestors emigrated from Germany are thus expected to spread their picnics under the German flag and so on. Inside the memorial's museum a guest book registers visitors' comments. On a recent July day visitors from St. Paul, Seattle, and Kalispell, Montana, had already driven past Belgrade and noted that the Centennial Memorial was "interesting," "tasteful," and "well designed." Given its size the Belgrade park would have been impossible to place in town, but its location outside the city on a major highway indicates the solution that towns have found for their symbols. If the freeway takes the visitors past the town, then the symbol heads for land along the freeway. Rothsay's "Prairie Chicken" serves as a gateway to that town from its freewayside park as does Frazee's largest "Turkey" (the small "Turkey" stands downtown).

Since fiberglass was used originally for boats, there is certainly no reason why a town symbol shouldn't also float. Virginia's giant "Loon" and Albert Lea's "Mermaid" do just that. The "Loon" first appeared in 1979 on Silver Lake in Virginia.

It was designed by local artist Bill Martin who had to build a second bird in 1982 after his first loon was damaged. A *Land of the Loon Festival* in June centers around this symbol. Albert Lea's "Mermaid" (a Copenhagen lookalike) was built after members of the Danish Brotherhood decided that there ought to be something Danish in local parades. Their papier-mâché "Mermaid," coated with fiberglass, floats in Fountain Lake every summer when not used in parades.

Using fiberglass to preserve wood is another trick of the symbol trade. Near Bemidji's "Paul Bunyan and Babe" stands "Chief Bemidji," carved of wood under a fiberglass coat. It is the second "Chief Bemidji" figure to stand in Library Park. The first, carved by Gustav Hinsch in the 1890's of inch-wide boards nailed together, stood by Lake Bemidji until it could no longer be repaired. The first "Chief Bemidji" figure had moved around town before being given to the city; this very eroded figure is now on display inside the Beltrami County Historical Society's museum. The second "Chief Bemidji," carved by Erik Boe in 1952, is made of cedar wood covered with preservative fiberglass.

The Rattvik "Horse" in Cambridge is another example of a figure carved in wood, but covered with fiberglass. The horse is one of several in central Minnesota which recall the area's Swedish immigrants, but all of the others are of the red "Dala" type. In Mora a giant Dala horse was built while a fiberglass Dala horse beckons customers to a Scandinavian giftshop in Cloquet. From the town of Rattvik in Sweden's Dalarna Province, 85 families came to settle in the Cambridge area and so it seemed appropriate to have the town's symbol not only be Swedish in form, but Swedish in manufacture. Bengt Larrson of Rattvik made the horse by the traditional method of wood layers glued together. It was painted blue grey with tiny black and brown dots and pinwheels on its chest and flanks. The seven foot eight inch "Horse," dedicated in 1990, stands in Rum River Park, linking Cambridge with its sister city in Sweden.

Although Montevideo, Minnesota, was not settled by persons from Uruguay it does have a sister city relationship with that South American capital. As a result one of the state's more unusual bronze statues stands in Montevideo's mall. A small plaza midway through the mall is the site for a bronze statue of "General Jose Gervasio Artigas" (1765–1850), the national hero of Uruguay. The Artigas figure is the work of Juan Blanes, the famous Uruguayan painter. The original, cast in Italy in 1898, stands in Uruguay; casts were made in 1949 for Montevideo, Minnesota, and Washington, D. C. Artigas is shown in battle dress, one hand grasping the hilt of his sword. The statue arrived in time for *Fiesta Days* in 1949 and continues to be part of Montevideo's annual celebration each June.

Sculptures can emphasize cultural and historic links between countries as the "Rattvik Horse" (1990) of Cambridge does. The wooden horse was constructed in Sweden as a "Celebrate Minnesota 1990" project.

Towering above the highway across from Ironworld, USA, is Chisholm's "Iron Man," an eighty-one foot tall composition honoring the major industry of Northern Minnesota. Jack Anderson's miner, all thirty-six feet of him, holds a shovel and stands on a base of Cor-ten steel whose shapes suggest the ways of forging American steel. The steel frame of the figure is covered with copper and bronze sheets, a construction method similar to that used for "Hermann" in New Ulm.

Silver Bay, too, honors miners with their statue of "Rocky Taconite" (1964). Rocky was made of quarter inch steel plates by a Minneapolis firm and placed on a chunk of taconite. After years spent by a mall, the figure was moved to a more visible location next to Silver Bay's welcome sign in August, 1990.

Farther north in Menahga, people of Finnish descent felt they needed something to remember their past, and so St. Urho was born. There were rumors, at first, that this hitherto unknown saint had saved Finland, but what he had looked like or done was a mystery. So there was a contest in 1975 and "a true likeness" by local artist Rita Seppala, was chosen. Her drawing became the model for a chainsaw carving by Jerry

In 1949 the city of Montevideo, Uruguay, sent two casts of Juan Manuel Blanes' statue of "Jose Artigas" (1898) to the United States: one to Washington, D. C. and the other to Montevideo, Minnesota. The Liberator of Uruguay stands in Montevideo's mall, sometimes with a plastic bottle nestled in the hilt of his sword.

Ward, which was placed on its pedestal in 1982. Ward's figure, carved from a laminated oak block, shows St. Urho, the patron saint of vineyard workers, proudly holding a grasshopper on the end of his pitchfork. Grasshoppers, after all, were the nasty creatures which the good saint had banished from the vineyards with his incantation of "Heinasirkka, Heinasirkka, menetaalta hiiteen" (Grasshopper, grasshopper, go away). Unfortunately, the oak figure did not last so a replica in fiberglass was made by F.A.S.T. in 1988.

Jerry Ward's chainsaw carving is but one among many which are now found in Minnesota (see Chapter Six). Many were commissioned as town symbols like Barnum's "Lumberjack" by Dennis Roghair, a very elongated "Viking" in Milan by Wendell Olson, a "Bald Eagle" in Wabasha by Jim Smits, Kathleen Reitan's "Steamboat Captain" in Carver, or the "Trout" by Barry Pinske outside the city hall in Preston. One group, however, seems to bring the story of town symbols full circle. In May, 1991 a committee interested in reviving Brainerd's downtown put on an arts festival. Several chainsaw carvers were commissioned to complete carvings during the two days of the festival. The subject was "Paul Bunyan Tales." Each figure represented a stage in Paul's life (such as his babyhood or schoolboy days) or another character in the legends. The group of Bunyan figures stands in what is to be a new park on Laurel Street, attesting to the continued strength of the mythical logger's hold on Minnesota's imagination and his role as a town symbol.

The twelve foot tall plate steel figure of "Rocky Taconite" (1964) stands on a taconite rock next to the sign for Silver Bay. The modern miner was erected by the Village and Reserve Mining Company. Photograph courtesy of Patricia Clogston.

6 "Let the Chips Fall Where They May"

Paul Bunyan swung a mighty axe, but no one so far suggests that he carved any awesome statues. Certainly a lot of Minnesotans have carved, whittled, or sawed their way through logs of cedar, oak and pine. Immigrants brought with them carving traditions for furniture, toys, and religious art such as altarpieces. Probably the state's earliest outdoor wooden figures were shop signs such as the cigar store Indians (discussed in Chapter One). Weathervanes, whirligigs and decoys were other early and now collectible works by carvers. The entertainment world brought another form of commercial woodcarving to Minnesota: the merry-go-round or carousel.

Two early carousels still enchant riders although neither is in its original location. The Minnesota State Fair carousel, built in 1914 by the Philadelphia Toboggan Company, was dismantled and readied for the auction block in 1988. Folk art collectors and museums have become interested in carousels. *The New York Times* article by Rita Reif noted that a complete carousel had recently been sold at auction for $693,000 and a carousel greyhound for $59,400, which was then a record price (*The New York Times*, September 20, 1987). The State Fair carousel nearly met that lucrative fate. A committee, called Our Fair Carousel, organized to buy it so that it would remain in Minnesota, was successful at the last moment. With funds from local donors and the city of St. Paul, the carousel was repaired and moved to an indoor location on a landing above the garden at Town Square. The sixty-eight horses prance on what is now known as the Cafesjian Carousel after the major donor to the fundraising appeal.

In its heyday from 1880 to 1930 the usual location for a carousel was in the amusement park at the end of the trolley line. Excelsior Amusement Park, on the western shore of Lake Minnetonka, was home to another Philadelphia Toboggan Company carousel. The park opened in 1925 and closed forever after the summer season of 1973. The Excelsior Carousel was given to the new Valleyfair Amusement park in Shakopee, which opened in 1976. The Excelsior Carousel has 48 animals and several chariots (Marling 1990).

The image of a carousel is of circles of horses, either fixed or moving up and down ("jumpers"). Other exotic animals such as lions, tigers, sea serpents, giraffes, ostriches, pigs, and the swan chariots were carved, but were never as common. A truly unusual carousel is currently being carved in the small town of Kellogg, just north of Winona. The three dozen animals have been designed by Donn Kreofsky and are being realized in basswood or butternut. There will be the traditional horses, but an ostrich, a Vietnamese pot-bellied pig, a sea turtle, a moose, three goldfish, a hippopotamus, and a sea horse will join them when the L.A.R.K. (Lost Arts Revived by Kreofsky) carousel is completed.

Several branches of the National Woodcarvers Association unite Minnesota's professional and avocational woodcarvers. Members of the Viking Chapter (located in the Twin Cities) exhibit their work twice a year and often give demonstrations at fairs and festivals such as the Minneapolis Aquatennial. A thirty foot tall cedar pole carved by chapter members during the 1975 Aquatennial was displayed briefly in front of the Northern States Power building at 5th Street and the Nicollet Mall. It was then permanently placed in a park near the Nicollet Island Inn. Design squares on the three sides of this pole represent ethnic and national groups present in Minneapolis; each square was signed by the carver.

Another Viking chapter pole was donated to a KTCA television fundraising auction. It was purchased for the Indian collection of the Thunderbird Motel in Bloomington, where it still stands. That pole was designed by Bill Butterfield and carved by members of the chapter.

Although these poles are often referred to as "totem poles," they do not display clan or family symbols in the Native American fashion. More accurately called "heritage poles," their designs include portraits, scenes, and objects relating to the theme of each pole. In Blackduck Jim Schram and other woodcarvers created an eagle topped heritage pole in 1984. Blackduck has held a well attended wood carvers festival every July since then.

Raymond Duhaime, who was part Indian and part French, carved several "story poles" incorporating nontraditional images such as a deer whose tail ends in peacock feathers. After Du-

haime retired to live in Grand Portage he sought training in Ojibwe crafts. His teachers were two elders, Mrs. Spruce and Mrs. Tamarack. From them he learned how to make birchbark containers, how to do quillwork, beadwork and hooked rugs. His wood carvings and baskets were sold in area shops. The Cook County Historical Society commissioned him to carve a cedar figure for a park at the entrance to Grand Marais. His "Pierre the Voyageur" carries a paddle and wears a large square canoer's pack on his back.

The carving of wood with hand tools is a centuries-old traditional art and practised worldwide. The use of power tools for carving is much more recent. The chainsaw, whether electric or gasoline powered, came along after World War II when the rapidly expanded housing market called for faster methods of cutting trees. Chainsaw sculpture is said to have begun in the Pacific Northwest among lumberjacks already adept with the tool. From Washington, Oregon, and Northern California it spread east to Minnesota by the 1970's. Chainsaw carvers demonstrated their craft at fairs and later in competitive carve-ins. During *Tall Timber Days* in Grand Rapids in August, 1991, chainsaw sculptors competed for the title of International Champion. Each man was given a six foot trunk of white pine supplied by the Blandin Corporation. For the next six hours each man was expected to create an eagle from his log. Judges then selected the winner. The 1991 champion, Gary Patterson of Waterloo, Illinois, carved the winning eagle and did it during an all day rain. Chainsaw sculptors usually wear protective headgear as well as goggles and gloves; for this competition they needed boots, ponchos and rainpants as well.

Eagles with outstretched wings, formed from the "Y" of a tree, bears, fish, and lumberjacks are favorite subjects for chainsaw carvers, but the range of subject matter is steadily expanding. Vikings, sea captains and soldiers all stand on stumps of elm or oak. Ash, cedar, elm, oak and pine are all woods used by carvers, but cottonwood is avoided, as it tends to rot. At the Minnesota State Fairgrounds in St. Paul, John Hunter was first hired in 1983 to carve figures from the dead elms. Before he hung up his chainsaw and moved to Michigan, Hunter had finished clowns, acrobats, a chicken, and a chef for a total of ten sculptures in all. There were more dead trees at the fairgrounds, however, so Dennis Roghair then took on the task in 1991. To date he has carved a "Standing Bear," a lawman ("Gonna Ride"), an Indian ("From his Bounty"), and a small boy in a Twins T-shirt looking at the waterslide ("Anticipation").

Although chainsaw sculptors carve freestanding pieces, they often take jobs carving stumps near their workshops. If the client wishes a figure carved from a tree on his own property, then obviously chainsaw and sculptor will travel and carve on site. Drawing up a carver's map would then suggest looking for carvings by Joe Mouldry near Olivia, for Wendell "Butch" Olson's work around Bird Island, Larry Jensen's sculpture in Brainerd, Jerry Faber's in Walker, John Gage's in Two Harbors, Dennis Weimar's near Stillwater, and the works of Terry Boquist and Ray Reitan south of the International Falls area. Some sections of the state appear underpopulated with chainsaw sculpture, but given the continuing growth and popularity of this form of art, that probably will not be the case for long.

Chainsaw equipment distributors, such as the Tilton Equipment Company, hire sculptors to demonstrate their products. Jerry Ward was showing what a chainsaw could accomplish one

In Milaca Dennis Roghair's chainsaw figures are found in Trimble Park, at the golf club, and downtown. "The Statue of Liberty" (1986) was carved for the Milaca town centennial in 1986.

For the Minnesota Veteran's Home in Hastings, Dennis Roghair did two chainsaw sculptures: an eagle and this World War I soldier.

day in Park Rapids when visitors from Menahga came by. They promptly asked if he would be willing to carve the St. Urho statue they had in mind. Ward carved the Saint using only the teeth of his chainsaw to demonstrate what could be done.

Once the figure is carved with a chainsaw and perhaps detailed with a chisel as well, it can be painted or stained and varnished. These surface treatments may need to be repeated annually. Or, the sculpture can be left to weather naturally to a gray color. Jerry Faber notes that most figures will split after a year and he cheerfully offers to split any of his figures for his customers if the wood doesn't do so naturally. Faber's workshop, located south of Walker, is filled with small and large works, finished and in progress. Faber's largest sculpture thus far measured thirteen feet, seven inches. These three whales were carved of elm as a gift for the Russian people for their help in saving the whales trapped under the ice at Point Barrow, Alaska. The large sculpture is now in Vladivostok, but a shorter prototype stands outside a giftshop on Highway 71 north of Bemidji.

Larry Jensen, like Jerry Faber, has a large studio and retail shop. Jensen's town symbols can be seen at Pequot Lakes, Grey Eagle, and Osakis. One of his largest works was done as a multilevel sign for the Birchwood Resort in Garrison. A group of seated fishermen occupy the base while above the resort's name another standing figure beckons tourists to enter. More recently he finished an eagle as a war memorial for the county court house in Aitkin.

Not all of Minnesota's chainsaw art has been done by residents of this state. The tall Indian head placed next to the information center in Two Harbors was part of Peter Toth's ambition to carve an Indian head in every state, a goal he finally achieved in 1988. A. J. Lutter divides his chainsaw work between Minnesota and northern California. Others, like John Hunter, Jerry Ward, and Terry Boquist, have left Minnesota and may no longer be doing chainsaw art.

Jon Strom, originally from Worthington but now resident in Bear Creek, is a sculptor and builder of log houses as well as a carver of chainsaw figures. For the town of Embarrass Strom did a group of four lifesize figures in white pine. The project was one supported by "Celebrate Minnesota" in 1990. Each of the figures represents a typical Iron Range occupation and each carries an appropriate tool. The pioneer woman heads for the well with her dipper, the logger has a crosscut saw, the miner has his pick and the farmer holds high his rake. In 1991 Strom added figures of two children to the pioneer group.

Strom's figures are realistic with close attention paid to details of dress such as buttons and pockets. As Willard Moore pointed out in his essay for the *Circles of Tradition* catalogue, chainsaw carvers create public art which is viewed as "practical, natural, realistic and fitting" (Moore 1989: 19). Sometimes the tree seems to fit the project. When a fir tree died on the grounds of St. John's Lutheran Church in Lake Elmo, its lower branches spread straight out horizontally instead of reaching upwards. Church members felt the tree "begged to be a Jesus," so that is what Dennis Weimar carved for them. Chainsaw carvings

of religious figures are not common, but another figure of Christ is now being carved by Chris Effrem on the grounds of St. Mary's Greek Orthodox Church in Minneapolis.

Most, but not all chainsaw carvers are self-taught. Some how-to books and video lessons in carving exist, but most carvers learn by doing. Increasingly they sign their works or attach metal labels to them, although Jerry Faber says that only "artists" date their works. Increasingly, too, chainsaw carvers are producing more sophisticated work. Not only are the details of dress accurate, but bodies are no longer rigid as if still imprisoned in the tree trunk. Although bears and eagles seem to be the most common subjects, perhaps the choice of animals carved will also change over time.

Terry Boquist's "Jackpine Savage" stands in a small park in Littlefork. This stock character from logging legend sports one of the most luxuriant mustaches in captivity.

7 Cast in Concrete: Fine, Folk, and Folly

Setting something in concrete sounds final, permanent, definite and very solid. As a medium for outdoor sculpture concrete seems a perfect choice as it can be cast in a mold or applied as a layer of stucco over an armature of wood or welded metal. Reliefs and figures in the round are thus possible to create in concrete. Before it hardens other objects can be inserted, giving the finished sculpture either a rough texture or a glittering surface from shards of glass. Concrete sculptures do chip and break under stress. If they are painted (like "Paul Bunyan" and "Babe the Blue Ox" in Bemidji) they will need to be repainted every few years.

Working with concrete has appealed to many Minnesotans from traditional fine art sculptors to builders of town symbols and folk art environments; their works can be seen throughout the state. Students of one sculpture class learned how to build the inner supports and form a work in concrete. Their "Bear Tree Column," completed by students in Raymond Gormley's class, still stands in a park on Grand Marais' waterfront. It was a gift to the city from the Grand Marais Art Colony in 1953.

Two Minnesotans were early winners of the prestigious Prix de Rome, granted for study in Europe. Paul Manship won it in 1909 and Joseph Kiselewski of Browerville was awarded the prize in 1926. Kiselewski studied at the Minneapolis School of Art and then worked in Lee Lawrie's New York studio for four years before winning the Rome prize. Most of the artist's career was spent in the east, but he returned to Browerville for the last years of his life. In an interview Kiselewski commented that his own favorite work was a bronze figure of "Peace" commissioned by the United States Battle Monuments Commission for a military cemetery in Margraten, Holland (*Little Falls Transcript*, October 15, 1980.)

After Kiselewski had returned from Europe, the pastor of a Browerville church had an idea. Members of St. Joseph's Catholic Church (now called Christ the King Catholic Church) would soon be celebrating the fiftieth anniverary of the parish. Using materials left over from the construction of a new parish school, Father John Guzdek had built a mound to suggest the Mount in the Garden of Olives. What was needed, Father Guzdek thought, was outdoor sculpture and in Joseph Kiselewski Browerville already had its own nationally recognized artist. Kiselewski modelled a group consisting of a kneeling Christ whose prayers and gaze are directed towards a standing angel. The figures were cast in concrete by a New York firm and placed on Father Guzdek's rock mound.

At the time the Kiselewski group was dedicated the newspaper in Todd County's largest ci-

The figures of "Christ" and "The Angel" (1932) were designed by Joseph Kiselewski for the rock mound outside of Christ the King Catholic church in Browerville.

more angels are placed on the next, lower wall. The walls were built by Edward and Donald Feia of Holdingford who used over 500 loads of field-stone donated by local farmers. Plaques along the walls gave the names of servicemen as this was to be a Soldier's Shrine. At the dedication, Governor Harold Stassen remarked that it was the first such shrine to honor "the men of the armed forces fighting in this war" (*St. Cloud Daily Times*, September 8, 1942).

Another fieldstone grotto and shrine which was inspired by the grotto in Lourdes, France, was built in the tiny town of Two Inlets, north of Park Rapids. Father Joseph Moylan thought his hillside looked like Lourdes but needed a grotto, so in 1959 the parishioners of St. Mary's Catholic Church began building. In the stone grotto are marble statues of the Virgin and St. Bernadette; along the hillside under the pines are separate stone Stations of the Cross. Recently sculptor Ray Wattenhofer, who lives across the street, designed and built a series of waterfalls and pools measuring fifteen by thirty feet, alongside the grotto.

Until very recently visitors to St. Paul could have visited St. Michael's Apostolic Church and Grotto at 376 Rose Avenue on the city's east side. The church itself was quite tiny, measuring eighteen feet long by twelve feet wide, and it no longer exists. It was built by Gabriel Pizzuti in 1934 in memory of his daughter. Worshippers could attend services in a fully equipped sanctuary. The WPA guide to Minnesota listed the church and grotto as worth visiting; it was later described as St. Paul's only folk folly (Gebhard and Martinson 1977: 97). It was demolished in the late 1980's.

Concrete figures have long served the needs of promotion and advertising. As town symbols such figures promote seasonal festivals and tour-

ty ran a long article about the church, its history, and its hardworking pastor. Father Guzdek, the paper commented, used "only his brain and rocks" (*Long Prairie Leader*, September 1, 1932). Not far away in Holdingford there were also a lot of rocks and a pastor with the desire to build a shrine. Reverend John Komolicki, the pastor of St. Hedwig's Catholic Church, suggested his plan for a lot opposite the church to Reverend Gilbert Winkelman, dean of the school of Architecture at the College of St. John's in Collegeville, who designed the shrine. On the tallest wall of the shrine is a statue of Christ the King. Angels with trumpets stand at each end of this wall while two ism. "Paul Bunyan" and "Babe the Blue Ox" of Bemidji, "Lucette Diana Kensack" of Hackensack, the Vergas "Loon," Mora's "Horse," Wheaton's "Mallard," the "Pelican" of Pelican Rapids, and the "Otter" of Fergus Falls have already made their appearance in these pages, but there are others more directly linked to the promotion of a place rather than a town.

Perhaps the oldest of such place symbols is "Princess Owatonna," the guide to the healing waters of Mineral Springs in Owatonna. An Indian Princess was supposedly restored to health by drinking the water so her concrete effigy points the way. When the city of Owatonna decided to stress camping in a city park they asked a local contractor, William Berghs and his son Larry, to build both a fountain and the statue of the Princess in 1931. Until 1986 the Princess stood on her platform next to Maple Creek. Then the creek overflowed, damaging the figure. After the statue had been repaired, "Princess Owatonna" was placed across the road from the creek, farther away from potential water damage. A large wooden sign stands next to the statue explaining the legend of the curative waters.

The legends of Paul Bunyan are usually said to have come to life in the writings of W. S. Laughead and James Stevens. Paul's adventures had begun in lumberjack tales earlier told in Pennsylvania, Michigan, Texas and Montana, but only became famous in the promotional pamphlets published in 1914 and thereafter by W. S. Laughead for the Red River Lumber Company of Akeley. Later James Stevens added his legends to the canon. The cast of characters usually includes Paul, Babe the Ox he nursed to health following the winter of the Blue Snow, Johnny Inkslinger the bookkeeper, Sourdough Sam the cook, and others. Robert Frost gave Paul an un-

"Princess Owatonna" (1931) still points the way to the health giving waters of Mineral Springs, but from a vantage point out of harm's way.

named girlfriend in his poem, "Paul's Wife," and Doad Schroeder imagined a girlfriend almost Paul's size, later to be named "Lucette." But in Brainerd Paul's wife was Pauline.

Fifteen years before the Paul Bunyan Amusement Park opened, Brainerd held a *Paul Bunyan Water Carnival*. For that first event, held in July, 1935, the Bunyans were everywhere; Paul with his axe and Pauline with her cast iron skillet. The carnival committee organized parades, a pageant, and sports events, hoping townspeople would support the project by growing Bunyanesque beards or planning other related activities. Gas station owner Art Lyonais decided to commission a statue of Paul and Babe. The artist is unknown (he was said to have been a transient who lived under a Brainerd bridge), but his concrete figures still stand next to Realty World on south Sixth Street. Originally they stood farther back from the street in front of the tourist cabins. Realty World's owner Loran Knack had the pair moved and says they function admirably well as a place marker for his business. "People may not be able to find south Sixth Street, but they all know where Paul Bunyan is," he said. The "Paul Bunyan" and "Babe" of Sixth Street have been repainted and are now protected by a fence, befitting their status as the state's oldest statue of the mythological logger and his friend.

Changing attitudes sometimes end a statue's usefulness as an advertising symbol. Early in his career Halvor Landsverk, the woodcarver of Highland, made many concrete figures which he displayed for sale on his front lawn. (Later he returned to carving the Norwegian chair or "Kubbestol.") An Indian figure by Landsverk was purchased in the early 1950's by Clarence Prohaska for use at Mystery Cave. Landsverk's figure wears a fringed shirt and leggings, an eagle feather bonnet (the feathers are made of galvanized metal windmill fins), and a hairpipe breast plate. In its left hand it carries a pipe while it raises its right hand in greeting. When the statue was placed in front of the cave, a group of Winnebago Indians from Albert Lea asked if they could name and dedicate the statue in honor of their leader, Chief Decorah. For many years the Winnebagos returned each year to celebrate the memory of Chief Decorah at Mystery Cave. When the Minnesota Department of Natural Resources took over Forestville State Park and Mystery Cave the Chief's days were numbered. In an article in the *Spring Valley Tribune* the manager of the park said that statues didn't belong in natural settings and what could be considered a stereotype of an Indian might offend Native American visitors. He also felt that the dress of the figure was not that of the Sioux who were native to the area (*Spring Valley Tribune*, January 11, 1989). "Chief Decorah" was advertised for sale. The figure was purchased by the City of Spring Valley which arranged for its display next to the town's tourist information center on Highway 16.

Resort owners in northern Minnesota decided that a permanent sign of some sort was needed to show the way to Lake Kabetogama. What was built on Highway 53 became a tourist attraction in its own right. The base holds the sign which says "Lake Kabetogama Walleye." Above that the sixteen foot long concrete walleye seems to leap through invisible waves. Behind the sign is a staircase so that visitors can climb up, sit in the saddle and ride the walleye, creating their own versions of tall-tale postcards. ("See the fish I caught, even rode, and then threw back!") Duane Beyers from Cook, Minnesota, built the walleye in 1949.

Loggers and especially the greatest logger of

them all, Paul Bunyan, have their fame in Northern Minnesota, but equally legendary were the much shorter Voyageurs. The loggers cleared the forests while the French voyageurs were navigating the many lakes of the Boundary Waters in search of trade. The voyageur's garb of deerskin leggings and moccasins, tasseled cap and braided sash appears on several Minnesota statues: the fiberglass men of Crane Lake and Cloquet and the voyageur of wood at Grand Marais. At twenty feet in height, Two Harbors' "Voyageur" stands as tall as Bemidji's Paul; his concrete stucco body is formed over telephone poles. His eyes can move and his head turns so he can watch tourists passing the motel he guards on Highway 61.

While Halvor Landsverk was active in the business of making concrete figures, each of the other statues mentioned is the only effort known by that particular person. Other sculptors who chose concrete for a medium were far more prolific. Ernie Konikson's works can be found in several northwestern Minnesota towns. He came originally from Erskine where his "World's Largest Northern" stands in a park by Lake Cameron. In front of the Win-e-mac Motel on Highway 2 outside Erskine is his Indian lady carrying her baby in a cradleboard on her back. East from Erskine is his walking lion in McIntyre's Roholt Park while along Highway 59 heading south are a dog and, in Winger, a polar bear and seal. The biggest of Konikson's works is "The Pembina Trail Monument" in front of the Red River Val-

"Chief Decorah" (c1940) once greeted visitors outside Mystery Cave. Halvor Landsverk's figure now stands next to the Tourist Information booth in Spring Valley.

Joe Rolette walked many miles behind many ox carts in his time. "The Pembina Trail Monument" (c1965) by Ernie Konikson stands in front of Crookston's Red River Valley Winter Shows building in his memory.

ley Winter Shows Building in Crookston. For that monument Konikson made a concrete Joe Rolette walking behind a Red River cart pulled by an ox. A plaque on the cart notes that the gigantic three piece statue grouping was designed, created, and constructed by E. S. Konikson, "the Vagabond of the Rockies."

Konikson's sculptures were commissioned by chambers of commerce or Lions' clubs and they function as town symbols. The "Santa Claus Town" built by Bernard Swanson was intended as a roadside tourist attraction. Swanson mixed characters from Mother Goose and Walt Disney with other images drawn from popular culture. His concrete attraction was purchased by Cletus Dunn in 1960 and moved to land adjacent to Dunn's service station on Point Douglas Road

south of St. Paul. Professor Rob Silberman selected Swanson's "Blue Parrot" for inclusion in an exhibit called "Critic's Choice" held at the Minneapolis College of Art and Design Gallery in 1987. Silberman wrote in a brief catalogue essay that the Swanson pieces were in poor condition and deserved conservation as interesting examples of folk art. As the disintegration has unfortunately continued the "Santa Claus Town" may not survive for long.

Carl Peterson's sculpture was also chosen by Silberman for the exhibition at MCAD. Peterson was a blacksmith who once lived near St. James where he built twenty-four figures of concrete molded over iron armatures. When he moved to a nursing home in St. James the figures went with him. They were later purchased by

McIntosh's "Lion" (1960) was created by Ernie Konikson for parade use by the local Lions club. Later it was placed in Roholt Park.

Gerald Czulewicz, an antiques dealer from Bethel. Most have since been sold, but at least one figure, a standing bear, was exhibited in the "Circles of Tradition" folk art show.

Peterson's people and animals, now dispersed, are part of what is apparently a very widespread folk art phenomenon. Walker Art Center exhibited objects from several American folk art environments in "Naives and Visionaries" (1974), but the urge to create in concrete is far more widespread. In France it is considered "Art brut"

Ernie Konikson's "Indian Lady" carries her child in a cradleboard on her back. The figure is located at the Win-e-mac Motel east of Erskine.

or raw, outsider art. As Allen Weiss noted in an article entitled "In Europe, Tracing the Art of the Outsider" (*The New York Times*, November 20, 1988) artists and museums collect it and there are now a number of books dealing with outsider artists and their works. Weiss described several important sites where concrete sculptures have been preserved: the Abbe Fouré's carved cliffs at Rotheneuf near St. Malo, the Palais Ideal built by postman Ferdinand Cheval in Hauterives, south of Lyon, and La Maison Picassiette in Chartres, created by Raymond Isidore. Each of these French sites is being preserved and maintained, a problem which arises with all folk environments once the original artist has died.

Sculpture gardens with concrete figures have a fairly long tradition in the Far East. As Roger Warner wrote in "Asian sculptors made the meaning of life concrete," (*Smithsonian*, March, 1991) the Tiger Balm gardens of Hong Kong and Singapore have been tourist attractions for over fifty years. Warner wrote about two newer gardens of concrete sculptures built by a Laotian artist named Boun Leua Sourirat. One garden is in Laos, the other in Thailand near the village of Nong Khai. In both gardens the mix of Hindu and Buddhist imagery serves both religious and moral purposes. Proper behavior is exemplified by concrete figures of the good and the damned.

In the United States folk environments with didactic programs exist in many locations from Georgia to Kentucky, Kansas, Wisconsin, and California. Some are being preserved by groups organized for that purpose. Some have also been listed on state or national historic registers. Groups like the Kansas Grass Roots Art Association and California's SPACES (Saving and Preserving Arts and Cultural Environments) have led the research in documenting these en-

vironments. And in Wisconsin the Kohler Foundation has granted funds towards preserving environments such as the Paul and Matilda Wagner Grotto near Sparta, Wisconsin.

In Minnesota several folk art environments exist, all but one privately owned. All were essentially yard displays that grew and expanded on the owner's property. There, again with one exception, they remain. As their names suggest ("Itasca Rock Garden," "Scenic Rock Garden," and "Aksarben Gardens"), their builders considered them as gardens filled with flowers and rock-studded concrete structures. All welcomed visitors. In most of the communities where they were built, the neighbors considered the gardens as an asset to be visited.

The folk gardens to be discussed here are "Itasca" near Albert Lea, Arco, "Molehill" in Sauk Rapids, and "Aksarben" at Bay Lake. The "Itasca Rock Garden" was built by John Christensen (1875–1939) on land between what was known as the old Robert Wedge home and the Itasca village school near County Road 101. Promoters of the village of Itasca to be the county seat of Freeborn county lost a bet on a horse race to the supporters of Albert Lea. The Christensen garden lies in the center of what was once Itasca and is now greater Albert Lea. Fields nearby contain the plants and flowering trees of Wedge Nurseries.

When Christensen bought the house in 1925 he began his rock garden. On the south end an artificial hill provides the base for his largest castle and conceals a storage shed. Underneath the castle is a room where he kept garden supplies and equipment for his beehives. A smaller castle stands at the north end, completing the garden. In between are paths, bridges, niches, nooks, pools and seating areas, all made from concrete, rocks and bricks. There were fountains, water-

The tallest buildings of John Christensen's "Itasca Rock Garden" (1925–1938) were built on an artificial hill. Underneath the castle were storage rooms and connections for electricity and water.

falls, and flowers everywhere. Once his garden was complete, Christensen began building again, but this time it was an indoor rock garden with a pool constructed in the basement of his house. A rock wall plaque carries the date of 1938. The following year Christensen died.

His widow kept the property until 1950 when it was sold to the Arthur Johnsons. They maintained the rock gardens and are probably responsible for many of the plantings. One of the pools was filled in during their tenancy after one of their five children almost drowned in it. Through the years the gardens became a popu-

lar tourist destination and backdrop for wedding and graduation photographs. The property is now owned by Joseph J. Spark, Jr., who hopes to restore both the indoor and outdoor rock gardens.

An article in the *Albert Lea Tribune* (June 15, 1986) noted that Christensen and his wife brought back rocks from their travels, especially geodes, stalactites and rocks of unusual shapes, to incorporate in the garden. The Pedersens of Arco, Louis Wippich of Sauk Rapids, and the Vogts of Bay Lake were all savers of interesting rocks as their gardens show.

Arco is a small community in Lincoln Coun-

ty, five miles east and south of Ivanhoe, the county seat. H. P. Pedersen (1885–1942) started his rock and concrete constructions on his farm. When he purchased the Arco gas station in 1936 other stones he had collected were put to use in decorating the facade of the building. An adjacent building, also rock-covered, held a guest book for visitors to sign. Pedersen and his son Vernon then built a "Scenic Rock Garden" with a miniature village. After World War II, Vernon (b1912) added more buildings to the small scale village and started doing large size sculptures. In 1952 the gas station was sold and Vernon Pedersen left Arco. Many of the thirty-five sculptures were either sold or moved to other Pedersen family homes; only the rock-covered station (still privately owned) and four statues still remain. The "Statue of Liberty", "Hugo the Ram," the "Scenic Rock Garden" sign, and the "Liberty Bell" were moved to Anderson Park on the west shore of Lake Stay. Some of the rocks and shiny chips are missing today, especially from the crossed flags on the base of the "Liberty Bell" and from the hillock on which "Hugo the Ram" stands, but at least something remains in Arco of the Pedersens' work.

Louis Wippich (1896–1973) designed his "Molehill" towers and garden, but local teenagers helped him build it. The material was granite; the pillars, posts, walkways, and bridges took twenty-four years to build on Wippich's lot in Sauk Rapids. Ted and Karon Sherarts wrote that Wippich found his stone materials at local monument

"Hugo the Ram" (1946–1952) was moved to Anderson Park on Lake Stay after Vernon Pedersen left the town of Arco.

companies and quarries. Wood and metal came from "condemned freight cars" in the Great Northern railroad shops. The belief system of Theosophy guided Wippich's life and influenced the structures of "Molehill." Wippich died in 1973 but the last structure built in "Molehill" was finished in 1958 (Sherarts and Sherarts 1974). In contrast to the other rock environments described in this chapter, and perhaps due to the materials employed, Wippich's structures are tall and lean. His two towers or "mountains" rise thirty and forty-five feet, respectively, bristling with granite spikes. At Itasca, Arco and Aksarben the scale is smaller, the heights are lower, the texture encrusted, not smooth, the aesthetic totally different. Yet, "Molehill" too, was intended for others to visit and perhaps to use. "Molehill" is currently privately owned and appears to be well-maintained.

"Aksarben Gardens" was the name given to the house and land on Tame Fish Lake owned by Hugo and Arnold Vogt. "Aksarben" is not only Nebraska spelled backwards, but the name given to Omaha's leading philanthropic society. The Vogt brothers wintered in Omaha, but spent their summers in the house east of Bay Lake on County Road 14. They had purchased the land in 1917 and began the custom of spending summers near distant Vogt relatives.

The Vogt brothers specialized. Arnold (1890–1955) was the gardener and flower show judge; Hugo (1875–1956) was the builder. After eighteen summers of work their land held rock towers, a castle with a moat, a wishing well, a garden with a waterfall and a statue of a nymph (slightly resembling Harriet Frishmuth's nude dancing girls), and hundreds of flowers. Summer tourists staying at nearby resorts came to visit and eventually were required to pay twenty-five cents each to a coffee can. Part of the attraction at "Aksarben Gardens," one former Bay Lake resident recalled, was the brothers themselves. Dressed in striped "Iowa" bib overalls and barefoot, they showed visitors through the gardens, sometimes offering samples of their home baked bread. By ringing a bell at the boat dock, they could summon bass for treats and thus "Long Lake" became known as "Tame Fish Lake" in honor of their achievement. An interview with the brothers in 1936 noted that they had built three rock bridges, an Indian village, a grape arbor and a sign which read "Eveless Paradise" (Archives, Crow Wing County Historical Society). Pages in their guestbook (kept under a stonework canopy) once showed the names of Clark Gable, Norma Talmadge, and Will Rogers as visitors in the 1930's when "Aksarben" was still being completed. Following the Vogts' deaths, "Aksarben Gardens" was owned and maintained as a tourist attraction by Rose and Rudy Seliga until 1975 and then by Gretchen and Jerry Finnerty until 1979. The original six acres have now been sold, divided, and are no longer open for visits. Many of the original stone structures remain and the Finnertys run a nursery, also named Aksarben Gardens, on part of the property.

"Aksarben," "Itasca," "Arco," and "Molehill" all took decades to build. During the lifetimes of their builders they were well known locally and perhaps even regionally. Postcards published in the 1930's and 1940's by Curt Teich of Chicago, L. L. Cook of Milwaukee, and others illustrate "Aksarben" and "Itasca," and this probably helped spread their fame. Although none of these environments may yet be old enough for designation as state or national historic sites, perhaps in future years such recognition could help protect these examples of Minnesota's folk arts.

8 Temporary Sculpture: Here Today, Melted Tomorrow

For a brief period of time some sculptures appear on Minnesota's cultural landscape. Here today, perhaps to remain for a few hours or days, and gone tomorrow. Storage may be the destination for works which will be back at the same time next year while others, truly site-specific, disappear forever. Obviously, these temporary sculptures are not included in the Listing of Outdoor Sculptures at the end of this book, but they should be summarized nonetheless.

Parades call into being numerous examples of temporary sculpture. For nineteenth century parades honoring completion of railroad lines temporary arches were erected over the streets of Minneapolis and St. Paul. Floats carry papier-mâché or fiberglass figures which may be reused or their components cannibalized for later constructions. St. Paul's Winter Carnival and Minneapolis' Aquatennial have daytime and evening parades with many floats carrying temporary sculptures. Such floats are mechanized and need to conform to regulations and restrictions in size and on materials.

One parade, however, is still propelled by people power. Its participants walk through Minneapolis jointly or singly supporting giant sculptures and masks. This is the annual May Day Pa-rade, organized by In The Heart Of The Beast Puppet and Mask Theater for the past seventeen years. The parade route leads south on Bloomington Avenue to 34th Street where everyone turns to enter Powderhorn Park. Puppetbearers and paraders then spend the rest of the day watching performances and enjoying picnics on the hillsides surrounding Powderhorn Lake. The May Day festival always has a theme related to ecological or political concerns. Some of the giant puppets appear in HOBT plays, but many are newly created each year in puppetry workshops. In 1991 the parade story was called "Return to Turtle Island," referring to various Native American legends about the creation of the world.

Minnesota's winter festivals have long included ice carving and snow sculpting contests. For the winter season of 1991–1992 either ice or snow sculpture contests were planned for winter festivals at Worthington, Grand Marais, Grand Rapids, Lindstrom, Duluth, Cottonwood, Isle, Fulda, and Palisade (*The Minnesota Explorer*, Winter, 1991–1992.) For the 1991 Winter Carnival in St. Paul the ice carvers were professionals who could use power tools. Their works were carved and displayed in Rice Park, watched over

Giant puppets and masks are hoisted aloft for Minneapolis' May Day parade. Each year these symbols of the mythical and natural world, created under the direction of In the Heart of the Beast Puppet and Mask Theatre, march down Bloomington Avenue for eventual display in Powderhorn Park.

by Sir Windchill, a giant inflatable penguin and corporate logo of the North Star Ice Company, the sponsor of that event. In other years professional ice carvers from the Soviet Union, Japan and China were invited to St. Paul to demonstrate their skills during the Winter Carnival.

Snow sculpting for St. Paul's Winter Carnival in 1991 was done by teams of amateurs who received kits of hand tools including an axe and shovel. Each team was provided a ten by six foot block of snow. Their results were displayed along Constitution Avenue next to the ice slide on the Capitol Mall.

The largest work of ice at the St. Paul Winter Carnival is the home of its king, Boreas Rex. In their book, *Ice Palaces* (1983), Fred Anderes and Ann Agranoff devote two chapters to St. Paul's Winter Carnival castles. The first three palaces, built between 1886 and 1888, were the largest. Each had a large central tower, walls several feet thick with turrets and gates, and ice sculptures. These palaces were built to be occupied during the weeks of carnival activities. Concerts, balls and even a wedding took place inside the glimmering and lighted rooms. Locations for the palaces were in Central Park (downtown) and on Harriet Island. The palaces for the carnivals of 1896 and 1916–1917 were smaller, lower stockaded forts, rather than castles; these were located in Rice Park or Harriet Island.

When the Winter Carnival began again in 1937, after a lapse of twenty years, the palaces built were sometimes only screens or backdrops. By the time of the centennial of the Ice Palace in 1986, the concept of the palace as a residence for the Ice King was gone. Safety concerns and insurance limitations made entrance to the palace impossible for the general public. Instead of

A patriotic hand waving a flag was carved in snow for the 1991 St. Paul Winter Carnival. The armless hand (reminiscent of the Addams Family's "Thing") was the work of Terry and Jeanne Labelle and Tom Pnewski.

wandering in and out of many rooms as carnival-goers were able to do a century ago, those who went to Lake Phalen to see the Ice Palace could only walk around the perimeter. The Ice Palace had become virtually an ice sculpture, enduring only until the forces of the Fire King, Vulcanus Rex, attacked it and the walls of winter collapsed. But, as Larry Millett wrote, even though building such a structure seemed to some "a chilled folly," the Ice Palace was a community effort built by hundreds of volunteers. For its brief lifespan the Ice Palace became a symbol of community effort and pride, a temporary town symbol of winter in St. Paul (*St. Paul Pioneer Press and Dispatch*, February 7, 1986). The following year a stone monument in the shape of that Ice Palace was placed on the west shore of Lake Phalen, north of the Picnic Pavilion. It honors the project and carries the names of the numerous donors and volunteers. The highest pinnacle of the 1986 Ice Palace was 129 feet. For 1992 the Palace will tower over 150 feet and be located at Harriet Island where, planners hope, Super Bowl visitors will come to admire it.

At county fairs and especially at the Minnesota State Fair butter sculpture has long been demonstrated. After sculpting the not yet finished Minnesota state capitol in butter for the Pan American Exposition in Buffalo in 1901, John Karl Daniels made annual appearances as a butter sculptor at the State Fair (*Minneapolis Journal*, March 1, 1923).

Daniels could carve in ice as well as in butter. When the French First World War hero Marshal Ferdinand Foch made a visit to St. Paul in 1921, Daniels was asked to carve a bust of the marshal from a block of ice. He managed this feat in Rice Park in a fast four hours watched by a large crowd (*St. Paul Daily News*, November 26, 1921). Had Marshal Foch arrived in August, his bust probably would have been done in butter.

Another unusual and temporary medium for sculpture was available in Austin in 1991. The Geo A. Hormel Company celebrated its centennial with a "Spam Jamboree Day." Guests were invited to eat and sculpt the company's most famous product. As one reporter wrote, there were some "fair likenesses of Rodin's 'Thinker' sculpted in Spam" (*The New York Times*, May 20, 1991.)

Holidays bring out other forms of temporary decorations and sculptural assemblages. Such "assemblages," as noted in the recent *Circles of Tradition* catalogue, are part of Minnesota's contemporary and popular folk art scene. As Halloween increasingly becomes an adult celebration, bedsheet ghosts, carved jackolanterns and hay stuffed figures in lifelike poses appear in yards.

Christmas at many homes means a wreath, a few strings of outdoor lights and perhaps garlands of evergreens around the front door. Carolers, nutcracker soldiers, Santas, snowmen, and nativity scenes in plastic, glowing with inner lights, take up residence in other yards. Commercially produced figures share the holiday spaces with homemade figures. In Wayzata John Hunter's chainsaw figure, known as "The Wizard," is dressed in red garbage bags for temporary service as Santa Claus. Light displays often become a neighborhood project as residents of entire city blocks decide that every house should deck its roofs, windows, doors and trees with twinkling colors.

Yard displays during other seasons vary from minimal gardens to shrines or collections of figures and animals. In a recent "Peanuts" comic strip Lucy sneeringly looked at Charlie Brown's snowman and asked, "But is it art?" Makers of snowmen are probably less concerned with such questions than with whether the "right" accessories (hats, scarves, and carrots for noses) are available.

Yard displays include shrines, which often use a small figure of the Virgin in a rock grotto. A St. Paul black artist, however, created temporary shrines which were well known local landmarks in the 1970's. Maurice Carlton (1909–1985), a retired railroad worker, placed his store window shrines along Selby Avenue in St. Paul. Two of his best known outdoor sculptures were signs, the "Mother Love Shrine" which once stood in the community garden at Selby and Dale and the weather vane which hung on the Inner City Youth League building at Selby and Victoria Avenues. Both signs are now in the collection of the Minnesota Historical Society (Connolly 1988).

Scholars of popular culture have been interested in what is assembled in a yard display, who the makers are, and whether ethnic background or geographic location affects what is so often painstakingly arranged (Sheehy 1988, Schroeder 1977, Thompson 1990). In yard displays handcarved items may be juxtaposed with the commercially produced or with items reassembled from found objects. Displays grow to fill the space as time and energy are available.

In his essay for the exhibition *Black Art. Ancestral Legacy*, Robert Farris Thompson discusses what he terms "Yard-shows and Bottle Trees." Thompson suggests the following components for the yard shows he has surveyed: rock boundaries, porch mirrors, jars and vessels, motion-emblems, cosmograms (diamonds or circles), flowers planted within tires, sculptures of animals or people, trees hung with shiny bottles, swept-earth yards, graveyard decorations, and plantings of protective herbs (Thompson 1990: 123–124). White-washed rock boundaries, cast cement figures, flowers planted within tires, and the motion emblems are all found in Minnesota yard displays. The motion emblems, as Thompson lists them, are wheels, tires, and moving objects. Minnesotans choose wagon wheels (often as boundary markers or gates), and whirligigs to suggest motion and perhaps pioneer days as well.

Some yard display artists stop when their gardens and figures seem complete. Others continue. Their richness and exuberance make such yards local attractions. The front and side yards of Mike Schack's home in Grand Rapids are filled with flowers, handmade or store bought decorations and his figures of Popeye, Olive Oyl, and the Giant Mosquito. Schack's yard is clearly intended for others to enjoy as were those of H. P. and Vernon Pedersen, Carl Peterson, Hugo and Arnold Vogt, John Christensen and Louis Wippich (all discussed in Chapter Seven). Yet as yard displays are private creations their future survival will always be in doubt. They are longer lasting, certainly, than ice, snow or parade sculpture, yet they may still be ephemeral creations since the next owner of the yard may not be interested in maintaining the display.

The sculpture and fountains found in Minnesota's parks would not seem at first glance to be temporary installations, yet in some aspects they are. When the weather turns cold and the water must be turned off in the fall, some foun-tain sculptures go into hiding. The Heffelfinger and Phelps fountains in the Minneapolis Rose Gardens, the Berger fountain in Loring Park, and the Schiffman fountain with its large mermaid in Como Park, are all boxed up until spring.

Floral displays like Como Park's "Gates Ajar" begun in 1894 by Frank Nussbaumer, are obviously seasonal and temporary. "Gates Ajar" with its 15,000 flowers is a favorite setting for wedding photographs. The popularity of "Gates Ajar" even led to a replica. At the State Fairgrounds John Hunter carved a chainsaw bridal couple who stand in their own floral display next to the Agricultural and Horticultural building.

Fountains are clearly presented to cities for permanent use. However, vandalism, deterioration, and urban renewal change the permanent display to temporary and sometimes to the category of lost forever. John Karl Daniels carved a granite fountain for the Griswold family in memory of their son, Lewis. The fountain stood in Summit Park until someone decapitated its central figure of a boy, so the remnants of the work were removed to storage. A fountain figure of "Aphrodite" (Number 304 in the J. L. Mott Iron Works catalogue of 1905) once stood in Rice Park. It was later moved and displayed in Como Park. Today, the whereabouts of "Aphrodite" and a zinc alloy replica of Giovanni da Bologna's "Mercury" (once located in the Como Park Rose Garden) are unknown. And another fountain, the water veil built to honor William Hamm, Sr., stood in Hamm Plaza until 1990 when it was demolished. A new work of art designed by Jackie Ferrara will take its place.

For forty years Paul Manship's "Indian Hunter and his Dog" (1926) ran over the tiles of Cochran Park at Summit and Western Avenues in St. Paul. The work was commissioned for that space by members of the Thomas Cochran family in memory of their father. But after the arrows which the hunter carries were broken and obscenities were sprayed over the work the Department of Parks and Recreation decided to move the hunter and his four Canada geese. The new location was the McKnight Formal Garden, adjacent to the Conservatory in Como Park. In 1983 Robert Johnson made a fiberglass replica of the Manship group for display in Cochran Park.

Recently residents of the Ramsey Hill neighborhood where Cochran Park is located began a campaign for the return of the original Manship figures to the Summit Avenue location. They argue that Ramsey Hill is once more an elegant neighborhood and the Manship sculpture will be safe. As of this writing the matter has not been decided. Proponents of the move argue that the "Indian Hunter" was designed for Cochran Park and belongs there. Those in favor of the McKnight location say that there is more protection for the work in Como Park and that more people will see it there (*Minneapolis Star Tribune*, December 9, 1991). When the artist heard that there were plans to move the work in 1965, he wrote to businessman Ben Storey, "It seems silly to have a piece of sculpture boxed for 8 months! Very unattractive! It should go to the Conservatory!" (Letter, October 13, 1965. Files of the Department of Parks and Recreation). Manship died the next year, but it is clear from his letter that, wherever the statue is placed, he hoped that the temporary winter cover would not be used and that his sculpture would be permanently on view.

9 Corporate Art and Sculpture Gardens

Many Minnesota companies have art collections. Collections noted in the *Artnews International Directory of Corporate Art* (1988) include those of twenty-four Minnesota firms. Perhaps beginning with a portrait of the founder or the first president, they have branched out to collect prints, photographs, paintings, textiles, sculpture, and even African or Native American art. Railroads serving Minnesota, such as the Northern Pacific and Great Northern, commissioned art for use in advertising to encourage tourism along their routes. The paintings, prints, drawings and sculpture owned by the Burlington Northern, successor company to the Northern Pacific and Great Northern Railroads, have been shown in such exhibitions as *Iron Horse West* (1976) and *After the Buffalo Were Gone* (1985). Corporate art collections usually begin their displays in the lobby and continue through hallways, boardrooms, offices and inner courtyards. Only a few companies, however, collect or display sculpture outdoors. The problem is not taste or cost, but space. A company whose home office is built without a setback lacks a front yard for display. Newer buildings have large lobbies or atriums, but such spaces seldom offer room for many large pieces of sculpture.

Along the northern edge of the Minneapolis downtown is a major display of modern architecture punctuated by sculpture. On the Nor-

west Operation Center's corner at Second Avenue and Third Street is Mark di Suvero's giant red "Inner Search," one of three works by this artist in Minneapolis. Underneath the curtain wall Federal Reserve Bank Building is a spillway, home to Dimitri Hadzi's "Arcturus," Charles Perry's bright yellow "Thrice," Paul Granlund's "The Time Being," as well as to skate boarders. The Federal Reserve's corporate collection began with the commissions for these works in 1970. On the west side of the Northwestern National Life building are Masayuki Nagare's granite shapes.

This concentration of corporate art will now be joined by a series of artworks set in and on the redesigned Nicollet Mall. Business owners along this major mercantile artery recently funded a complete redevelopment of the outdoor mall. Commissions for art were awarded to Stanton Sears, Kate Burke, Seitu Jones and TaCoumba Aiken, Kinji Akagawa, George Morrison, Carl Nesjar, Philip Larson and Elliot Offner. Larson's etched glass walls have been installed in the Mall's eight transit shelters. The art glass designs evoke various art and archaeological styles known in Minnesota. Each of the other projects also suggest the state's flora, fauna, and other natural features from the bronze heron, loon and sage grouse of Offner's "Fountain" to the granite mosaic walkway designed by George Morrison. The

Nicollet Mall's art collection is expected to be in place by the fall of 1992.

When the Nicollet Mall was first developed in 1967 few works of sculpture were displayed. Jack Nelson's "Sculpture Clock," the H. C. Richardson granite fountain, and the glittering stainless steel "Tetraedros" sculpture by William Severson and Saunders Schultz in front of the IDS Center were the only permanent examples of such art for many years. The clock and "Tetraedros" will remain but the fountain, dedicated in 1967 by Mrs. Lyndon Johnson and Mrs. Hubert Humphrey, was demolished before redevelopment began.

Builders of indoor malls, beginning with Southdale in 1954–1956, have commissioned sculpture for their huge indoor courtyards. Since all of these sculptures are located inside they are not included in this guide. The space once given to these sculptures appears to have dwindled over the years as the courtyards fill with other displays and portable gypsy vendor carts.

Smaller shopping centers and office parks usually lack sculpture, but one developer decided otherwise. Samuel Marfield and his partners hired Russell Erickson to design sculptures for a number of his centers in the western suburbs of Minneapolis. Erickson used steel rods and wire for his large abstract compositions. Usually his name, the title of the work, and many happily roosting birds can be found on these sculptures. Conceived on a large scale, the designs were intended to be seen and "read" quickly by drivers on the freeway. The artist says his own favorite is "Starlight Moonlight" because of the way light reflects on its surface.

The two largest outdoor corporate sculpture collections are not located downtown. Honeywell, Inc. expanded its headquarters in 1978 and an unneeded parking area became a small park. The following year Harry Landes' "24 Elements" became the initial purchase for this outdoor display area. Over the years works by Kenneth Snelson and Robert Murray were added to Honeywell's Park just off 24th Street. Additions, however, are no longer being made to the collection. Two of its works, Scott Burton's "Seat-Leg Table" and Mark di Suvero's "Molecule," have been given to the Walker Art Center, where they will be placed in the Minneapolis Sculpture Garden.

General Mills' sculpture garden was not started immediately after the corporate headquarters moved from downtown Minneapolis to Golden Valley in 1958. It was nearly a decade before the company began to commission sculpture for its new rolling 85 acre campus. Of the works now on view only Richard Serra's "Core" had already been completed; all of the remainder have been designed for the site. Curator Don McNeil says the company prefers to give artists the freedom to try something new in size or material. Jackie Ferrara, for example, who is well known for her work with milled cedar, used limestone for her "Stone Court," which is set above the entrance pond. Artists are encouraged to develop projects which employees can use. Scott Burton's concrete "Picnic Table" seats up to twenty, Philip Larson's "Medusa's Head" is made of walkable concrete paving blocks and Richard Fleischner's granite patio surrounded by evergreens is intended to be entered. Even the walk from the parking lot to the employee's entrance is aided by art as Siah Armajani's covered walkway, all 695 feet of it, offers that possibility.

Minnesota's hospitals also collect art for some of the same reasons businesses do. Art enhances the premises, perhaps softens a hard business image or warms an antiseptic medical facil-

The two spiral forms of John Newman's "Torus Orbicularis Major" (1988) are joined on a hilltop in the General Mills Sculpture Garden. The work is made of cast and fabricated aluminum.

ity. Collections of contemporary art suggest that the company is in touch with modern life; art for a hospital lobby or entrance offers symbols of hope, compassion, and sympathy. Hospitals, or their governing boards, seem more apt to commission figural rather than abstract or minimal art, at least for their outdoor sites.

One location for sculpture at a hospital is a small island in the center of the driveway. Paul Granlund's "Bethesda Angel" (for Bethesda Hospital in St. Paul) and his "Wellspring" (for

Abbott-Northwestern Hospital in Minneapolis) occupy such islands. Evelyn Raymond's "Legacy," created for the seventy-fifth anniversary of Fairview Riverside Hospital in Minneapolis, has a similar location. Other locations for sculpture in hospital settings are interior courtyards and the outer walls of the building.

When the Mayo Building was erected for the Mayo Clinic in Rochester in 1954 art was considered integral to the architecture. Three artists (William Zorach, Abbott Pattison, and Ivan Mestrovic) were commissioned to do works for three sides of the building, using the theme of "Mirror to Man." Mestrovic's tense, struggling figure ("Man and Freedom") is still impressive; whereas, Zorach's "Man and Work" and Pattison's "Man and Recreation" groups seem somewhat lost. Additions to the original ten story clinic were made in the 1960's so that the building is now much taller than when the sculptures were first conceived and installed.

Gifts to the Mayo Clinic have included fountains by Carl Milles ("Shell Blowing Triton") and David Wynne ("Boy with a Dolphin"), both set by the Mayo Building. Barbara Hepworth's very impressive cut out sculpture, "Four Square (walk through)" stands south of the Harwick Building.

West of the Mayo hospital complex is St Marys Hospital. Malvina Hoffman's "St. Francis and the Wolf" stands in front of that hospital. In the hospital's courtyards are Mayo Kooiman's figure of Edith Graham Mayo and Charles Gagnon's "St. Francis and the Birds." Gagnon's heroic size saint is looking at a peaceful bird perched on his outstretched arm. Doves become the major element for Gagnon's "Peace Fountain" in downtown Rochester. Fifty-seven bronze doves touch wings in interlocking circles of the fountain, located on First Street S. W. The "Peace Fountain" was commissioned by the city as part of downtown redevelopment:

Three contrasting examples of sculpture at hospitals are Hillis Arnold's bronze cross high above the entrance to St. Joseph's Hospital in St. Paul, the bronze group of Indian, settler and priest, honoring Father Francis Xavier Pierz (1785–1880) at the St. Cloud Hospital, and Andrew Leicester's "Horton's Tree" for St. Joseph's Hospital in Brainerd. Leicester's work uses paving blocks in red and blue to create what can be

The contrasts of mass and space are clearly seen in "Four-Square (walk through)" completed by Barbara Hepworth between 1960 and 1969. The cast bronze was a memorial gift to the Mayo Clinic in 1977 from the family of Constantine P. Goulandris.

seen as patterns of lines, yet what is intended to suggest the course of blood through veins and arteries.

Leicester's works are often linked quite tightly through the use of myth and history to the function and significance of the location. For a Cincinnati park along the Ohio River he designed a sculptural environment incorporating steamboats, the river and pigs. Although the city was once known as "Porkopolis," there was angry opposition to the idea of stressing this part of the city's past. When the "Sawyer Point" sculpture was dedicated, the pigs (which were the works of Douglas Freeman) didn't seem that overpowering. In fact, the standing winged pigs were soon popular and celebrated on T-shirts, mugs, and cupcakes. Cincinnati had once again become, like it or not, "that pig place" (Chavez 1988). "Octal" was a labyrinth which Leicester designed for Cray Research Company, using binary language to spell the company's name. Made of redwood and concrete the water labyrinth became a favorite spot for employees. Every May a "Ducky Day" was held when toys were set afloat in the labyrinth. When the Company moved from Mendota Heights in 1990 "Octal" was deliberately destroyed in what the artist described as a "celebratory fire."

Sculpture from iconic to abstract can also be seen at Minnesota's houses of worship. Churches and synagogues frequently have some space, whether in front of or adjacent to their buildings, where a sculpture garden may exist. Norman Holen's "Christ and the Child," a very large terra cotta piece, stands in just such a courtyard at the Vinji Lutheran Church in Willmar. Others have inner courtyards where devotional or memorial pieces stand. The plain facades of contemporary churches provide appropriate

The third stele of Michael Price's "The Olivet Triptych" (1987) was inspired by the story of the Prodigal Son as told in Luke 15: 11–32. When the son returns home his father calls on the servants to bring forth the best robe. This bronze relief stands in a small garden in front of St. Paul's Olivet Congregational Church.

backgrounds for large sculptures such as Alonzo Hauser's "Christ" on the Evangelical and Reformed Church in St. Paul, Evelyn Raymond's "St. Augustine" on the Church of St. Austin in Minneapolis, or her sixteen foot "Shepherd Boy" on the Church of the Good Shepherd, also in Minneapolis. Worshippers enter that church through Paul Granlund's bronze panelled "Credo Doors." Granlund's "Birth of Freedom" bronze set in front of the Westminster Presbyterian Church is, in a sense, the end marker of the Nicollet Mall's art collection which begins on the north at the Federal Reserve Bank's plaza.

The idea of a garden in which sculptures take their places amidst trees, flowers, lakes, and fountains is an old one. Gardens of the rich and famous were designed with statues lining the promenades or serving as focal points for the paths. Parks and cemeteries were the earliest sculpture gardens in America, but museums are increasingly moving their art into outdoor galleries. For some institutions a sculpture placed near the entrance serves as a museum symbol to be stamped on visitor buttons, much as Nick Swearer's "Iguana" is used by the Science Museum of Minnesota, or Ernst Barlach's "Fighter of the Spirit" is used by the Minneapolis Institute of Arts.

A brick walled garden adjoining the entrance to the Owatonna Art Center is the setting for "Reflections" by Paul Granlund, "Spirit of Peace" by Charles Gagnon, "Winged Figure" by John Rood and other works. A small space south of the Arts and Science Center in St. Paul is the location for an untitled work by Steve Beyer and "Two Lines Oblique" by George Rickey.

Every sculptor who works on a large scale has a continuing exhibit of his work around his home or studio. Anthony Caponi is turning his sculpture garden into the Caponi Art Park. Twenty acres of very hilly land located on Diffley Road in Eagan have been home to this artist since 1950. His sculptures are located on knolls, hillsides, and along paths which he has traced and shaped. "Pompei," a relief sculpture composed of seventeen bronze panels, is set into one hillside, to be discovered as if one were digging for the dead through Vesuvius's fury. The Caponi Art Park, as envisaged, would not only be a sculpture garden, but would function as an arts center with a wide range of programs for the citizens of Dakota County.

When Martin Friedman, then the director of the Walker Art Center, looked out the front door of his museum towards the Minneapolis Parade Grounds, he saw an empty field filled with possibilities. Walker had already displayed some of its sculptures on the terraces of its building, but in the space across the street many more works of art could be on view. The Parade Grounds once held an armory and later formal gardens, but Friedman saw it as a future sculpture garden. In September, 1988 that wish came true as the Minneapolis Sculpture Garden opened to the public. The seven and one half acre garden was designed by architect Edward Larrabee Barnes with the assistance of landscape architect Peter Rothschild. The twelve million dollar project was financed by private donations and foundation grants. The Minneapolis Park and Recreation Board is responsible for security and maintenance, with the Museum taking charge of all art and educational programs.

The plan of the garden is geometric. The four plazas (or roofless galleries) each one hundred feet square are crossed by two wide allees or paths. The South to North path leads from the museum to the pond occupied by Claes Oldenburg and Coosje van Bruggen's "Spoonbridge and Cherry" fountain. En route visitors walk on Sol Le Witt's "Walkway" as they cross Vineland Place, entering the garden through the topless arch provided by Martin Puryear's pair of Cold Spring granite columns called "Ampersand." East to West the path leads from Siah Armajani's "Irene Hixon Whitney Bridge" to the Sage and John Cowles Conservatory. The central tower of the conservatory was built to accomodate Frank Gehry's "Standing Glass Fish." Armajani's blue and yellow "Bridge" contrasts truss and suspension bridge construction and gives pedestrians poetry (a poem by John Ashberry is set in bronze in the wooden floor of the bridge) to think about as they pass over sixteen lanes of traffic, from Loring Park to the Sculpture Garden.

When the Minneapolis Sculpture Garden opened, an exhibit called "Sculpture Inside/Outside" was part of the inaugural events. Temporary sculptures commissioned for that exhibition were set up in the garden as examples of its "outside" dimension. Each of the roofless galleries and the paths contain sculpture from the Museum's permanent collection as well as some works on extended loan. They range from older acquisitions by Georg Kolbe, Giacomo Manzu, Marino Marini, Henry Moore, Jacques Lipchitz and Isamu Noguchi to the new commissions. Visitors thus enjoy a wide range of sculpture from modern to minimalist. Over the years it is expected that other temporary installations and extended loans may vary the display.

Critical and popular reaction to the Minneapolis Sculpture Garden has been good. Paul Goldberger, the *New York Times* critic, wrote that it was "the finest new outdoor space in the country for displaying sculpture." Goldberger liked the conservatory, "the simple and elegant and powerful" design of the garden and Armajani's bridge, which he termed "an almost magical mix of the toylike and the monumental" (Goldberger 1989). That the public also liked the garden was made clear by the busloads of visitors who came, estimated at 500,000 in the first year.

The success of the Minneapolis Sculpture Garden led to thoughts of expansion. By the spring of 1992 the garden will grow to ten acres. A stainless steel arbor supporting flowering vines, a granite floored sculpture plaza, flower beds, shade plants and walkways will fill this new area to the north of the present garden. The Scott Burton and Mark di Suvero works given to the Walker by Honeywell, Inc., will also be placed in the additional space.

Although sculptures in many styles stand in the Minneapolis Sculpture Garden it is somewhat fitting that the two largest works, "Standing Glass Fish" and "Spoonbridge and Cherry," are colossi. While the elegant garden and many of its other sculptures could be at home anywhere, a giant fish and a Paul Bunyan-sized spoon seem eminently suited for the state's largest collection of outdoor sculpture, truly monuments for Minnesotans.

Bibliography

Ames, Kenneth L. "Idealogues in Stone: Meanings in Victorian Gravestones," *Journal of Popular Culture* 14: 4 (Spring, 1981).

Anderes, Fred and Agranoff, Ann. *Ice Palaces*. New York: Abbeville Press, 1983.

Baker, Robert Orr. "Oakland Cemetery: A Safe and Permanent Resting Place," *Ramsey County History*, 16: 1 (1980).

Baruch, Mildred C. and Beckman, Ellen J. *Civil War Union Monuments*. Washington, D. C.: Daughters of Union Veterans of the Civil War, 1978.

Beardsley, John. *Art in Public Places: A Survey of Community Sponsored Projects Supported by the National Endowment for the Arts*. Washington, D. C.: Partners for Livable Places, 1981.

Blasdel, Gregg N. "The Grass-Roots Artist," *Art in America*, September-October, 1968, 24–41.

Boxmeyer, Don. "Big Stuff," *St. Paul Pioneer Press*, March 16, 1985. [Minnesota colossi.]

Bradshaw, Henry and Vera. "Roadside Gallery," *The New York Times*, May 31, 1959. [Minnesota colossi.]

Bullard, F. Lauriston. *Lincoln in Marble and Bronze*. New Brunswick, N. J.: Rutgers University Press, 1952. [Minneapolis Lincoln statue and the Pelzer Lincoln statues.]

Carlock, Marty. *A Guide to Public Art in Greater Boston from Newburyport to Plymouth*. Boston: Harvard Common Press, 1988.

Chavez, Lydia. "Debating the Fitness of Enshrining Swine," *The New York Times*, July 11, 1988. [Andrew Leicester's park for Cincinnati.]

Christenson, Kathryn and Miller, Kelvin W. *Paul Granlund, The Sculptor and his Work*. St. Peter: Gustavus Adolphus College, 1978.

Coen, Rena Neumann. *Painting and Sculpture in Minnesota, 1820–1914*. University of Minnesota Press, 1976. [Sculpture by Paul Manship and Jakob Fjelde.]

Coleman, Nick. "State's statues: A bit fishy, but mostly unforgettable," *Minneapolis Tribune*, August 22, 1982. [Minnesota colossi.]

Coleman, Nick. "Menahga Waits for Upstart Saint to be Finnished," *Minneapolis Tribune*, February 15, 1982. [St. Urho.]

Connolly, Loris. "Maurice Carlton and the Inner City Youth League: Something Good for the Soul," *Roots* 17:1, Fall 1988, 23–30.

Crease, Robert and Mann, Charles. "Backyard Creators of Art that says: 'I did it, I'm here'", *Smithsonian* 14:5 (August 1983) 82–91.

Cruikshank, Jeffery L. and Korza, Pam. *Going Public: A field guide to developments in art in public places*. Amherst, Massachusetts: University of Massachusetts Press, 1988.

Davidson, Martha. "Regional Review: Minneapolis — St. Paul 1943," *Artnews* XL1: 17 (January 15-31, 1943) 9–11.

Dennis, James M. *Karl Bitter, Architectural Sculptor. 1867–1915*. Madison: University of Wisconsin Press, 1967. [Thomas Lowry memorial in Minneapolis, pp. 204–220.]

Elrod, Sam. "Arts Project Left Mark," *St. Paul Pioneer Press*, October 8, 1972. [WPA art.]

Evert, Marilyn. *Discovering Pittsburgh's Sculpture*. Pittsburgh: University of Pittsburgh Press, 1983.

Folwell, William Watts. *A History of Minnesota*. St. Paul: Minnesota Historical Society, 1921–1930. 4 vols.

Fossum, Syd. "Prosperity Changes Art," *Minneapolis Star*, June 12, 1966.

Fried, Frederick. *Artist in Wood: American Carvers of Cigar-Store Indians, Show Figures and Circus Wagons*. New York: Clarkson Potter, 1970.

Friedman, Martin. *Noguchi's Imaginary Landscapes*. Minneapolis: Walker Art Center, 1978.

Friedman, Martin. *Sculpture Inside Outside*. New York: Rizzoli International Publications, Inc. and Walker Art Center, 1988. [Minneapolis Sculpture Garden.]

Garvey, Timothy J. "From God of Peace to 'Onyx John': The Public Monument and Cultural Change," *Upper Midwest History*, Vol. 1, 1981, 5-26. [Minnesota colossi.]

Gebhard, David and Martinson, Tom. *A Guide to the Architecture of Minnesota*. Minneapolis: University of Minnesota Press, 1977.

Glueck, Grace. "Sculpture Failing the Test of Weather," *The New York Times*, August 22, 1991, B2.

Goldberger, Paul. "Sculptural Links in the Chain of Urban Events," *The New York Times*, January 29, 1989, 33. [Minneapolis Sculpture Garden.]

Goldin, Amy. "The Esthetic Ghetto: Some Thoughts about Public Art," *Art in America* (May-June, 1974), 30-35.

Goode, James. *The Outdoor Sculpture of Washington, D. C. A Comprehensive Historical Guide*. Washington, D. C.: Smithsonian Institution Press, 1974.

Gutheim, F. A. "Civic Monumental Sculpture," *American Magazine of Art*, 26: 7 (July 1933), 371-379.

Hallam, John S., "Houdon's Washington in Richmond: Some New Observations," *American Art Journal* X: 2 (November, 1978) 72-80.

Hammond, Ruth. "It's easy to see why ducks stick in mind of Blackduck visitors," *Minneapolis Tribune*, October 20, 1979.

Hemphill, Herbert W., editor. *Folk Sculpture USA*. Brooklyn: The Brooklyn Museum, 1976.

Holmquist, June Drenning, and Brookins, Jean A. *Minnesota's Major Historic Sites: A Guide*. St. Paul: Minnesota Historical Society, 1972.

Jaeger, Luth. "Two American Sculptors. Fjelde — Father

and Son," The *American Scandinavian Review* X: 8 (Augusst 1922), 467, 472.

Johnson, Nancy A. *Accomplishments. Minnesota Art Projects in the Depression Years*. Duluth: Tweed Museum of Art, 1976.

Keillor, Garrison. "Thanks for Attacking the N.E.A.," *The New York Times*, April 4, 1990.

Kunz, Virginia Brainard. *Muskets to Missiles*. St. Paul: Minnesota Statehood Centennial Commission, 1958.

Lien, Dennis, "Blasphemy in Bemidji," *St. Paul Pioneer Press*, January 5, 1990. [Paul Bunyan and Babe the Blue Ox.]

Linker, Kate. "Public Sculpture: The Pursuit of the Pleasurable and Profitable Paradise," ARTFORUM, March 1981, 64-73.

Linker, Kate. "Public Sculpture II: Provisions for the Paradise," ARTFORUM, Summer 1981, 37-42.

Lipman, Jean. *American Folk Art in Wood, Metals and Stone*. New York: Dover Books 1972, (1st Ed., 1948). [Cigar-store figures and weather vanes.]

Margolies, John. *End of the Road*. New York: Penguin Books, 1981.

Marling, Karal Ann. "Minnesota Souvenirs. The large and the small of it," *Prospects* 11 (1987) 283-300.

Marling, Karal Ann. *The Colossus of Roads. Myth and Symbol Along the American Highway*. Minneapolis: University of Minnesota Press, 1984. [Minnesota colossi.]

Marling, Karal Ann. "Thrills and Nostalgia: The Amusement Parks of Hennepin County," *Hennepin County History*, Fall 1990, 49:4, 13-22.

Marling, Karal Ann. "She Brought Forth Butter in a Lordly Dish: The Origins of Minnesota Butter Sculpture," *Minnesota History* 50:6 (Summer 1987) 218-228.

Martin, Mary Abbe. "Tragic events, ironies inspire Twin Cities sculptor's work," *Minneapolis Star Tribune*, August 25, 1985. [Andrew Leicester.]

Martin, Mary Abbe. "Artists seek to humanize public work," *Minneapolis Star Tribune*, June 26, 1988. [Rodger Brodin, Siah Armajani, and Andrew Leicester.]

McCue, George. *Sculpture City: St. Louis*. Public Sculpture in the Gateway to the West. New York: Hudson Hills Press, 1988.

McGriff, Marilyn. "A horse of a different color," *Cambridge Star*, August 8, 1990. [Rattvik horse.]

McKinzie, Richard D. *The New Deal for Artists*. Princeton, N. J.: Princeton University Press, 1973.

Meier, Peg. "In Praise of Lumbermen," *Minneapolis Star Tribune*, July 21, 1990. [Rodger Brodin's "Lumberman."]

Millett, Larry. "Museum without Walls," *St. Paul Pioneer Press Dispatch*, September 4, 1988. [Minneapolis Sculpture Garden.]

Mitchell, Giles Carroll. *There is no Limit: Architecture and Sculpture in Kansas City*. Kansas City: Brown-White Company, 1934.

Moore, Charles. "Memorials of the Great War," *The American Magazine of Art* 10:7 (May, 1919).

Moore, Willard B., editor. *Circles of Tradition. Folk Arts in Minnesota*. St. Paul: Minnesota Historical Society Press for the University of Minnesota Art Museum, 1989. [Chainsaw sculpture and Halvor Landsverk noted.]

O'Connor, Francis V. *Federal Support for the Visual Arts: The New Deal Now*. Greenwich, Ct.: New York Graphic Society, 1969.

O'Connor, Francis V., editor. *Art for the Millions*. Greenwich, Ct.: New York Graphic Society, 1973.

O'Sullivan, Thomas. "Joint Ventures or Testy Alliance? The Public Works of Art Project in Minnesota, 1933-1934," *Great Plains Quarterly* 9: 2 (Spring, 1989) 89-99.

Proske, Beatrice Gilmer. *Brookgreen Gardens Sculpture*. Brookgreen Gardens, S. C., 1943.

Rand, Harry. *Paul Manship*. Washington, D. C.: Smithsonian Institution Press, 1989.

Roberts, Warren E. "Investigating the Tree-Stump Tombstone in Indiana," *in* Simon J. Bronner, ed. *American Material Culture and Folklife: A Prologue and Dialogue*. Ann Arbor: UMI Research Press, 1985, 135-153.

Robinette, Margaret A. *Outdoor Sculpture. Object and Environment*. New York: Watson—Guptill Publications, 1976.

Schroeder, Fred E. H. *Outlaw Aesthetics: Arts and the Public Mind*. Bowling Green: Bowling Green State University Popular Press, 1977.

Schmeckebier, Laurence E. "Sculptural Memories," *Northwest Life*, 18:7 (July 1945) 17-18 and 18:8 (August 1945) 20-21.

Schmeckebier, Laurence E. *Art in Red Wing*. Minneapolis: University of Minnesota Press, 1946.

Sheehy, Colleen J. "Giant Mosquitoes, Eelpout Displays, Pink Flamingos: Some Overlooked and Unexpected Minnesota Folk Arts," *in Circles of Tradition*. Minneapolis: Minnesota Historical Society Press, 1989, 45-59.

Somasundaram, Meera. "Chainsaw artist carves sculpture from trees," *St. Paul Pioneer Press*, May 21, 1990. [John Hunter.]

Stalker, Douglas, and Glymour, Clark. "The malignant object: thoughts on public sculpture," *The Public Interest* 66 (Winter, 1982) 3-34.

Steele, Mike. "On the Yahoo Trail in Minneapolis," *Landscape Architecture* 61: 4 (July, 1971.) [9 Artists/ 9 Spaces Exhibit.]

Von Sternberg, Bob. "Tall Tale. Paul's legend flows from an adman's prose," *Minneapolis Star and Tribune*, May 24, 1987. [Paul Bunyan and Babe the Blue Ox.]

Taft, Lorado. *The History of American Sculpture*. New York: The Macmillan Company, 1930.

Thalacker, Donald. *The Place of Art in the World of Architecture*. New York: Chelsea House Publications, 1980.

Thompson, Neil B. *Minnesota's State Capitol. The Art and Politics of a Public Building*. St. Paul: Minnesota Historical Society, 1974.

Thompson, Robert Farris. "The Song that Named the Land," *in Black Art, Ancestral Legacy*. New York: Harry H. Abrams, Inc. 1989, 97-141. [Yard displays.]

Tompkins, Calvin. "Open, Available, Useful," *The New Yorker*, March 19, 1990, 48-72. [Siah Armajani.]

Vick, Judy. "The Old Gray Corporation Ain't What She Used to Be," *Twin Cities*, September, 1981, 45-51, 102-104. [Corporate art collections.]

Wascoe, Don, Jr. "Swedish Sculptor upset by foam and

fiberglass copy," *Minneapolis Tribune*, December 16, 1974. [The Emigrants statue in Lindstrom.]

——. "Madison's Lou T. Fisk goes on Tour to Publicise Constitution Bicentennial," *Minneapolis Star*, February 22, 1987.

——. "Minneapolis Statues—a Dying Breed," *Minneapolis Tribune*, February 3, 1963.

——. *Naives and Visionaries*. New York: E. P. Dutton & Co., Inc., 1974. [See Ted and Karon Sherarts, "Louis C. Wippich. Clown of Molehill," 87–93.]

——. *200 Years of American Sculpture*. New York: Whitney Museum of American Art, 1976.

——. Federal Writers' Project, WPA. *Minnesota. A State Guide*. New York: The Viking Press, 1938.

——. *Forecast Chronicle*. Minneapolis: Forecast Public Artspace Productions, 1989.

——. *Walker Art Center: Painting and Sculpture from the Collection*. Mineapolis: Walker Art Center, 1990.

——. *Critic's Choice*. Minneapolis: Minneapolis College of Art and Design Gallery, 1987.

——. "Ak Sar Ben Gardens to close in September," *Aitkin Independent Age*, August 29, 1979.

——. *Process. A Sculpture by Stewart Luckman*. Minneapolis: University of Minnesota Art Gallery, 1981.

Listing of Outdoor Sculpture

The information for each sculpture is presented for each city, alphabetically by artist, in the following order:

Artist
Title
Dimensions
Location
Material
Donor or Sponsor

Birth and death dates, when known, are provided for each artist.

Following the Title is a date or dates indicating, when known: (a) date of original completion and/or (b) date of dedication, and/or (c) date of being moved to present location. The date an item was cast is indicated with the let-ter "c" and the date an item was moved to its present location is indicated with the letter "m". The abbreviation "ca." with a date indicates "circa".

Dimensions, when available, are provided in height, length, and then depth, generally in feet (with the symbol ′) but occasionally in inches (with the symbol ″). These dimensions are occasionally accompanied by the letters "H", "L" or "D", as appropriate. When a single number is listed without such a prefix, that number always represents the height. Dimensions for works exhibited by the Walker Art Center are given in inches.

The abbreviation "n.a." means that the information is not available.

The following abbreviations are also generally used:	
COMPAS	— Community Programs in the Arts
D.A.R.	— Daughters of the American Revolution
G.A.R.	— Grand Army of the Republic
MAC	— Minneapolis Arts Commission
Mn. DOT	— Minnesota Department of Transportation
MSF	— Minnesota State Fairgrounds
MSAB	— Minnesota State Arts Board
NEA	— National Endowment for the Arts
RUDAT	— Rural Urban Development Action Team
WAC	— Walker Art Center
WPA/MAP	— Works Progress Administration/ Minnesota Art Project
WRC	— Women's Relief Corps

Aitkin

Creative Displays
Blacksmith, 1981
12′
Aitkin Iron Works, 1st Street and 1st Avenue N.W.
fiberglass
Aitkin Iron Works

Jensen, Larry, b1954
Eagle, 1991
7′
Aitkin County Court House
wood, chainsaw, painted
Persian Gulf Support Group

Akeley

Krotzer, Dean, and others
Paul Bunyan, 1984
33′
Park, Main Street
fiberglass
Akeley Chamber of Commerce

Albert Lea

Bassett, George, b1929
The Danish Immigrant, 1981
10′
Lincoln Park, Ruble and Bridge Avenues
bronze
Danish Brotherhood

Christensen, John, 1875–1939
Itasca Rock Garden, 1925–1938
various
County 101, Itasca Road

rocks, brick, concrete
Artist

Perkins and Kratzert Company
Soldiers and Sailors Memorial, 1914
28'
Freeborn County Court House
bronze on granite
Various G.A.R. and WRC Posts

Stolp, Arthur, b1931
Christ, 1957
24' x 13'
Facade, First Methodist Church
brick relief
First Methodist Church

Alexandria

Dallman, Otto, b1907
Kensington Runestone [replica], 1951
25'
Highway 27 east of city
granite
Kiwanis

Shumaker, Gordon, b1920
Big Ole the Viking, 1965
28'
Broadway at 3rd Avenue
fiberglass
Runestone Foundation

Anoka

Brodin, Rodger M., b1940
Rick Sorenson, 1991
10'
opposite John Ward Park
bronze
American Legion Post #102

Brodin, Rodger M., b1940
King, 1988
3' x 2' 3"
King Park, Fairoak and Church Streets
bronze
Anoka Police department

Brodin, Rodger M., b1940
The Protector, 1987
3' 3" x 2' 3"
Police Department, 2015 1st Avenue N.
bronze
Anoka Police department

Arco

Pedersen, Vernon, b1912

Hugo the Ram, 1946-1952
7'
Anderson Park, Lake Stay
concrete, colored stones and rock
Artist

Pedersen, Vernon, b1912
Liberty Bell, 1946-1952
4'
Anderson Park, Lake Stay
concrete, colored stones and rock
Artist

Pedersen, Vernon, b1912
Statue of Liberty, 1946-1952
7'
Anderson Park, Lake Stay
concrete, colored stones and rock
Artist

Pedersen, Vernon, b1912
Scenic Rock Garden Sign, 1946-1952
L 12'
Anderson Park, Lake Stay
concrete, colored stones and rock
Artist

Arden Hills

Luckman, Stewart
[Untitled], 1975
various
Bethel College
Cor-ten steel
n.a.

Ashby

Moran, Steve
Giant Coot, 1991
10'
Highway 78, Coots Trap Range
concrete
Coots Unlimited

Austin

Artist Unknown
Soldiers and Sailors Memorial, 1906
15'
Oakwood Cemetery
bronze on granite
McIntyre Post 66, G.A.R., and WRC

Daniels, John Karl, 1875-1978
George Washington, 1937
7' 4"
Main Street and 1st Avenue N. E.

bronze
Judge & Mrs. Henry Weber

Barnum

Roghair, Dennis, b1953
Lumberjack, 1990
6'
City Hall
wood, chainsaw
Barnum Centennial Days Committee

Battle Lake

Creative Displays
Chief Wenonga, 1979
23'
Halverson Park
fiberglass
Battle Lake Civic and Commerce Club

Baudette

Lund, Arnold, [designer]
Willie Walleye, 1959
L 40' 4"
Park, at Highway 11
concrete stucco on iron
Baudette Civic and Commerce Association

Bay Lake

Vogt, Hugo, 1875-1956, and Vogt, Arnold,
    1890-1955
Aksarben Gardens, 1918-1936
various
Highway 14 between Aitkin and Bay Lake
rocks and cement
Artists

Beaver Bay

Gage, John, b1951
Beaver, c1987
10'
Highway 61
spruce, chainsaw
City of Beaver Bay

Belgrade

F.A.S.T. Corp.
Crow on Branches, 1990
18'
Belgrade Centennial Memorial, Highway 71
fiberglass
Centennial Committee, Celebrate Minnesota
    1990

Bemidji

Boe, Eric
Chief Bemidji, 1952
8'
Library Park, Paul Bunyan Drive
wood, chainsaw, fiberglass covered
Bemidji Jaycees

Dickenson, Cyril M.
Paul Bunyan, 1937
18' x 5'
3rd Street at Bemidji Avenue
concrete, plaster, paint
Bemidji Chamber of Commerce

Lofquist, Janet, b1952
Crosswater, 1990
various
Bemidji State College
bronze, granite, concrete
MSAB, Art in Public Places

Payton, Jim
Babe the Blue Ox, 1937
10' x 8'
3rd Street at Bemidji Avenue
concrete, plaster, paint
Chamber of Commerce

Big Falls

Boquist, Terry
Uncle Dan Campbell
10'
Park, at Highway 71
wood, chainsaw
Anonymous gift

Bigfork

Reitan, Ray
Lumberjack, 1989
15'
Village Hall, Highway 38
wood, chainsaw
City of Bigfork

Bird Island

Artist unknown
Our Lady of the Prairie, 1954
12'
St. Mary's Church, 10th Street
concrete
Church

Olson, Wendell "Butch", b1931

Indian, Eagle and Bear, 1987
15' each
Highway Avenue at 9th Street
elm, chainsaw
Private owner

Blackduck

Foley, Becky Balsiger, b1951
Black Duck, 1972
5' 1"
Drake Motel
wood, wire, papier mâché
Artist

F.A.S.T. Corp.
Black Duck, 1985
11'
Heritage Park
fiberglass
Local Committee

Schram, Jim
Heritage Pole, 1984
21'
Wayside Rest, Highway 71
wood, paint
Artist

St. Amant, P. J., and others
Black Duck, 1938
16' x 10'
Main Street and Railroad Avenue
wood
Blackduck Civic and Commerce Club

Blaine

Erickson, Russell, b1950
Nature's Inner Light, 1986
18' x 12' diameter
Springbrook Apartments
steel rods
Belgarde and Yaffe

Bloomington

Butterfield, Bill
Totem Pole, 1978
30'
Thunderbird Hotel, 2201 East 78th Street
cedar
Thunderbird Hotel

Creative Displays
Indian Brave, 1978
23'
Thunderbird Hotel, 2201 East 78th Street

fiberglass
Thunderbird Hotel

Creative Displays
Chippewa Man, 1982
15'
Thunderbird Hotel, 2201 East 78th Street
fiberglass
Thunderbird Hotel

Erickson, Russell, b1950
Starlight Moonlight, 1987
18' x 10' x 40'
Southtech Plaza, 9401 James Avenue South
steel rods
Marfield, Belgarde and Yaffe

Granlund, Paul, b1925
Familia, 1986
5'
Lifetouch National School Studios, Inc.
bronze
Company

Huntington, Charles, b1925
Untitled, 1978
18' x 6' x 6'
Normandale Community College
welded stainless steel, brass
MSAB, Art in Public Places

Johnson, Robert, b1922
Chief Thunderbird, 1980
9'
Thunderbird Hotel, 2201 East 78th Street
fiberglass
Thunderbird Hotel

Lofquist, Janet, b1952
What Lies Beyond, 1987
11' x 34' diameter
Minnesota Center, France Avenue at I494
granite, Cor-ten steel, cast iron
Homart Development Corporation

Blue Earth

Bassett, George, b1929
The Girl by the Pool, 1979
3'
Putnam Park
bronze
Local committee

Creative Displays
Jolly Green Giant, 1978
50'
Highways 90 and 169

fiberglass
Blue Earth Chamber of Commerce

Brainerd

Artist Unknown
Paul Bunyan and Babe, 1935
8'
1107 South 6th Street
concrete, painted
Art Lyonais

Bowen, Joe T.
Babe the Blue Ox, 1950
15' x 23'
Parking lot, Highways 210 and 371
fiberglass
Paul Bunyan Playground Association

Jensen, Larry, b1954
Bear with Painted Scarf
4'
3rd and Kingwood Streets
wood, chainsaw
Private owner

Leicester, Andrew John, b1948
Horton's Tree - Plaza, 1984
60' x 75'
St. Joseph's Hospital
colored concrete pavers
Hospital

Lutter, A. J.
Bear, 1991
8'
Laurel and 6th Streets
white pine, chainsaw
RUDAT

McVay, Pat
Paul Bunyan as a Baby, 1991
3' x 6'
Laurel and Sixth Streets
white pine, chainsaw
RUDAT

Reitan, Kathleen
Night Shift Chicken, 1991
7'
Laurel and Sixth Streets
white pine, chainsaw
RUDAT

Roghair, Dennis, b1953
Paul Bunyan as a Boy, 1991
7'
Laurel and 6th Streets
white pine, chainsaw

RUDAT

Watson, Dave
Paul Bunyan as a Schoolboy, 1991
7'
Laurel and Sixth Streets
white pine, chainsaw
RUDAT

Brandon

Artist Unknown
Relief [athlete and musician], 1935–1936
2'
Auditorium, 105 Holmes Street
concrete
WPA/ FAP

Browerville

Kiselewski, Joseph, 1901–1988
Christ and Angel in Garden of Gethsemani,
  1932
various
Christ the King Catholic Church
cement
Gertrude John

Cambridge

Larsson, Bengt
Horse [Rattvik style], 1990
7' 8" x 3' x 5'
Rum River Park
wood, fiberglass
Cambridge, Celebrate Minnesota 1990

Cannon Falls

Backus, Mrs. George J.
Colonel William Colvill, 1909
8'
Cemetery, Highway 19
bronze
Colvill Memorial Association

Carver

Reitan, Kathleen
Steamboat Captain, 1985
12'
Main Street at Broadway
elm, chainsaw
Carver Lioness Club

Cass Lake

Faber, Jerry, b1934
Logger, 1988

6'
Lyle's Logging Camp
wood, chainsaw, paint
Lyle Chisholm

Faber, Jerry, b1934
Logger and Eagle, 1991
15'
Cass Lake Library
wood, chainsaw, paint
Cass Lake Library

Castle Rock

Artist Unknown
Soldiers and Sailors Memorial, 1913
6' 2"
Valley Cemetery, Alverno Avenue
white bronze
Soldiers Memorial Committee

Chanhassen

Granlund, Paul, b1925
Winter & Summer Nymphs, 1973
6'
Minnesota Landscape Arboretum
bronze
n.a.

Huntington, Charles, b1925
Marcus Heffelfinger Memorial, 1988
6' x 4' x 3'
Minnesota Landscape Arboretum
welded stainless steel
Heffelfinger family

Leicester, Andrew John, b1948
The Wedding Tower, 1986
various
Minnesota Landscape Arboretum
wood
Minnesota Herb Society

Nash, Katherine, 1910–1982
[Untitled]
76" x 49" x 24"
Minnesota Landscape Arboretum
bronze, paint
Estate of Marjorie J. Howard

Chisholm

Anderson, Jack
The Miner, 1987
81'
Highway 169 near Ironworld USA
copper, brass, Cor-ten steel

Chisholm Bicentennial Committee, IRRB, City
  of Chisholm

Sabean, Samuel, b1902
Fountain of Youth, 1936
4'
Chisholm High School
stone
WPA/ MAP

Cloquet

Creative Displays
Dala Horse, 1978
11' 6"
Bergquist Imports, Inc. on Highway 33
fiberglass
Bergquist's Scandinavian Imports

Creative Displays
Voyageur, 1976
20'
Highway 33 near Tourist Center
fiberglass
Cloquet Bicentennial Committee

Collegeville

Breuer, Marcel, 1902–1981
Warner Palestra, 1971
15'
St. John's University
Cold Spring granite
Artist

St. Paul Statuary Company
St. Kater Tekakwitha, c1950, m1953
12'
Lake Sagatagan, St. John's University
cement
St. Olaf's Catholic Church

Columbia Heights

Caponi, Anthony, b1921
Mary, 1958
12'
Church of the Immaculate Conception, 4030
  Jackson Street, N. E.
Mankato limestone
Church

Crane Lake

Ed, Robert Bertil, b1920
Voyageur, 1958
13' 6"
Highway 24 and County Road 424

fiberglass
Crane Lake Commercial Club

Crookston

Konikson, Ernie, 1907–1977
Pembina Trail Memorial, c1965
15' x 50'
Red River Valley Winter Shows Building,
  Highways 2 and 75 North
concrete, paint
Private owner

Crosby

Creative Displays
Serpent, 1977
20' x 25'
North shore, Serpent Lake
fiberglass
Crosby Chamber of Commerce

Deerwood

Creative Displays
Leaping Stag, 1977
8'
Maple Road East and Front Street
fiberglass
Deerwood Civic and Commerce Club

Delano

F.A.S.T. Corp.
Chicken, 1990
11'
Unocal Service Station, Highway 212
fiberglass
Local committee

Delavan

Bassett, George, b1929
Delavan Pioneers, 1980
7'
City Park
bronze
Local committee

Detroit Lakes

Detroit Marble Company
Soldiers and Sailors Memorial, 1915
21'
Oak Grove Cemetery
Barre granite
WRC, G.A.R., Sons of Veterans

Duluth

Akagawa, Kinji, b1940
Four Seasons with a Sundial, 1986
20' diameter
Baptism River Rest stop
cedar, rock, steel, concrete
MSAB, Art in Public Places

Bartholdi, F. A., 1834–1904
Statue of Liberty, [replica 1949], 1976
8'
Harbor Drive, 5th Avenue West
bronze
Raymond Bartholdi

Bartlett, Paul Wayland, 1861–1925
Patriotism Guards the Flag, 1919
8'
5th Avenue West and 1st Street West
red granite
J. B. Culver Post, G.A.R.

Caponi, Anthony b1921
Wedging the Ashes of Time
22" x 31½"
University of Minnesota, Duluth, Sax Outdoor
  Sculpture Court
granite and steel
Tweed Museum of Art

Daniels, John Karl, 1875–1978
Leif Erickson, 1956
9'
Leif Erickson Park
bronze
Norwegian-American League

Doberfuhl, Donna
[Untitled sculptured wall], 1991
5' x L 75'
Canal Park Drive
brick
Duluth Public Arts Commission

Effington, Ben, b1951
Lake Superior Fountain, 1989
14' 6" x 20'
Superior and Lake Streets
India black granite, bronze
Duluth Public Arts Commission

Fairbanks, Avard T., 1897–1976
The Last Survivor, 1955, [cast 1983]
8'
Canal Park
bronze
Artist's family

Harper, Cynthia
[Five sidewalk medallions], 1991
1' 4" x 1' 4"
Canal Park Drive
bronze and ceramic
Duluth Public Arts Commission

Lipchitz, Jacques, 1891–1973
Daniel Greysolon, Sieur Duluth, 1965
9'
University of Minnesota, Duluth
bronze on granite
Bequest of Albert L. Ordean

Nardi, Dann b1950
Quarter of a Blue Moon, 1983
84" x 48" x 48"
University of Minnesota, Duluth, library
    entrance
cast concrete, steel rods
Tweed Museum of Art

Sears, Stanton, b1950
Siscowet Bench, 1990
1' 9" x 5' 8" x 12' 5"
Bay Front Festival Park
bronze
MSAB, Duluth Public Arts Commission

Shrady, Henry M., 1871–1922
Jay Cooke, 1921
10'
London Road and 8th Avenue East
bronze
Local committee

Tinsley Barry b1942
Cascade, 1986
11' 10" x 10' 4"
University of Minnesota, Duluth, near library
granite, aluminum, stainless steel
Tweed Museum of Art

Von Schlegell, David, b1920
The Gate, 1975
26'
Thompson Hill, I35 Rest Area
stainless steel
MSA Council, NEA

Eagle Bend

Quirt, Peter
The Eagle, 1983
3'
Highway 71 and Jackson Street W.
copper
Eagle Bend Centennial Committee

Edina

Erickson, Russell, b1950
Raker, 1978
22' x 14' x 7'
7760 East Bush Lake Road
steel rods
Samuel Marfield

Erickson, Russell, b1950
Free Form 1, 1973
21' x 15' x 7'
7401 East Bush Lake Road
steel rods
Samuel Marfield

Erickson, Russell, b1950
Wind Rods, 1977
20' x 7' x 24'
7700 East Bush Lake Road
steel rods
Samuel Marfield

Erickson, Russell, b1950
Red Horse, 1977
23' x 18' x 7'
5250 West 74th Street
steel rods
Samuel Marfield

Erickson, Russell, b1950
Reclined Figure, 1974
18' x 12' x 7' 6"
Marfield Industrial Building
steel rods
Samuel Marfield

Huntington, Charles, b1925
Untitled, 1970
24' x 24' x 24'
Metro Interchange Park
welded steel
Private owner

Embarrass

Strom, Jon, b1948
The Miner, 1990
6'
Embarrass-Vermillion Credit Union
wood, chainsaw
Celebrate Minnesota 1990 and local donors

Strom, Jon, b1948
The Farmer, 1990
6'
Embarrass-Vermillion Credit Union
wood, chainsaw

Celebrate Minnesota 1990 and local donors

Strom, Jon, b1948
Logger, 1990
6'
Information Center, Highways 135 and 22
wood, chainsaw
Celebrate Minnesota 1990 and local donors

Strom, Jon, b1948
Pioneer Woman, 1990
6'
Fire Department Well
wood, chainsaw
Celebrate Minnesota 1990 and local donors

Strom, Jon, b1948
Boy, 1991
4'
Information Center
wood, chainsaw
Celebrate Minnesota 1990 and local donors

Strom, Jon, b1948
Girl, 1991
4'
Information Center
wood, chainsaw
Celebrate Minnesota 1990 and local donors

Erskine

Konikson, Ernie, 1907–1977
World's Largest Northern, 1953
L 20'
City Park, Vance Avenue at 2nd Street
concrete, paint
private owner

Konikson, Ernie, 1907–1977
Indian Woman with Baby, c1970
8'
Win e Mac Motel, Highways 2 and 59
concrete, paint
Win e Mac Motel

Eveleth

Yackel, Ken
Tribute to John Mariucci, 1989
20' x 15'
Hockey Hall of Fame, Highway 53
bronze
Hockey Hall of Fame

Excelsior

Bakken, Vince

Pelican, 1983
5′
Excelsior Commons Park
wood, chainsaw
City of Excelsior

Freeman, Douglas, b1953
St. John the Baptist, 1982
8′
St. John the Baptist Church, 640 Mill Street
bronze
Church

Nash, Katherine, 1910–1982
Sails, 1980
6′
Excelsior Commons Park
stainless steel
Local committee

Faribault

Artist Unknown
Dog and Cat, 1937
3′ each
Pollard Hall, Minnesota School for the Deaf
Kasota limestone
WPA

Artist Unknown
Christ the Prince of Peace, 1944
6′
Library, Central Avenue and Division Street
concrete
Our Lady of Victory Circle, Daughters of
    Isabella

Nichols, Mark, b1954
Thunderbird, 1990
10′
Depot Square
painted steel
Paul S. Gray

Nielsen, Stuart, b1947
44 North, 1991
n.a.
Faribault Technical College
aluminum, painted
MSAB, Art in Public Places

Perkins and Kratzert Company
Soldiers and Sailors Memorial, 1914
7′
Rice County Court House
bronze
Cooke Post 123, G.A.R. and WRC

Whillock, Ivan
Bea Duncan Memorial Fountain, 1991
6′
Heritage Park
bronze, stone
Bea Duncan Memorial Committee and
    Celebrate Minnesota 1990

Fergus Falls

Hanley, Harriet, 1870–1962
George B. Wright, 1926
8′
Union Avenue
granite
Vernon Wright

Jaenisch, Steve, b1940
Canada Goose, 1990
L 23′
1110 Lincoln Avenue West
steel rods
Local committee

Jaenisch, Steve, b1940
Otter, 1972
L 22′
Adams Park, west shore Grotto Lake
concrete
Jaycees

Frazee

Scott, Shell
Big Turkey, 1986
22′ x 22′ x 16′
Lions Park, Highway 10
fiberglass
Frazee Community Club

Scott, Shell
Little Turkey, 1986
7′
Park, Lake and Main Streets
fiberglass
Frazee Community Club

Garrison

Creative Displays
Walleye, 1980
L 15′
Park, Mille Lacs Lake, at Highway 169
fiberglass
Garrison Commercial Club

Creative Displays

Robin Hood, 1983
15′
Sherwood Forest RV Park, Highway 169
fiberglass
Sherwood Forest RV Park

Glenwood

Kurtz, Mark, b1969
Eagle, 1991
5′
Pope County State Bank
wood, chainsaw
Pope County State Bank

Golden Valley

Armajani, Siah, b1939
Covered Walkway, 1988
L 685′
General Mills Sculpture Garden
steel, glass, wood
General Mills

Artschwager, Richard, b1924
Oasis, 1990
11′ x 12′ x 20′
General Mills Sculpture Garden
granite
General Mills

Beyer, Steve, b1951
P. H., 1977
65″ x 62″ x 62″
General Mills Sculpture Garden
steel
General Mills

Borofsky, Jonathan, b1941
Man with Briefcase, 1987
30′ x 13′ x 2½ ″
General Mills Sculpture Garden
Cor-ten steel
General Mills

Burton, Scott, 1939–1989
Public Table, 1987
various
General Mills Sculpture Garden
cast concrete
General Mills

Consagra, Pietro, b1920
Solid and Transparent Number One, 1968
12′
General Mills Sculpture Garden
bronze
General Mills

Ferrara, Jackie, b1929
Stone Court, 1988
8' x 65' x 24'
General Mills Sculpture Garden
limestone
General Mills

Fleischner, Richard, b1944
Untitled, 1987
18' x 24'
General Mills Sculpture Garden
granite, arborvitae
General Mills

Highstein, Jene, b1942
Egyptian Beauty, 1989
7' x 7' x 14'
General Mills Sculpture Garden
black granite
General Mills

House, John V.
Seed Pod, 1960
43" x 31" x 19"
General Mills Sculpture Garden
bronze
General Mills

House, John V.
Northwoods Staccato, 1970
4' 8" x 7' x 5'
General Mills Sculpture Garden
bronze
General Mills

Huntington, Charles, b1925
Scimitar, 1974
23'
General Mills Sculpture Garden
brass
General Mills

Huntington, Charles, b1925
Sunworshipper, 1971
20'
General Mills Sculpture Garden
painted steel
General Mills

Kendrick, Mel, b1949
Untitled, 1988
10' 6"
General Mills Sculpture Garden
bronze
General Mills

Larson, Philip, b1944
Medusa's Head, 1990

L 46' x W 5'
General Mills Sculpture Garden
concrete pavers
General Mills

Newman, John, b1952
Torus Orbicularis Major, 1988
10' x 12' x 15'
General Mills Sculpture Garden
cast aluminum
General Mills

Padovano, Anthony, b1933
Arc Segment, 1970
8' x 7' x 3'
General Mills Sculpture Garden
steel
General Mills

Serra, Richard, b1939
Core, 1986
14' 6" x 17' x 3' 2"
General Mills Sculpture Garden
Cor-ten steel
General Mills

Grand Marais

Duhaime, Raymond, 1909–1986
Pierre the Voyageur, 1975
6'
Wisconsin Avenue and Highway 61
cedar
Cook County Historical Society

Gormley, Raymond J., and others
Bears on a Column, 1953
21'
Bear Tree Park
concrete
Grand Marais Art Colony

Grand Rapids

Artist Unknown
Mannekin Pis, [1619], 1938
2'
Blandin Paper Company grounds
gilded metal
Charles Blandin

Schack, Mike
Yard Display, 1970 to date
various
1215 15th Avenue N. W.
wood, wire, plaster, rubber hose
Artist

Wattenhofer, Ray, b1948
Papermaker, 1985
8'
Pokegama Avenue at 2nd Street N. E.
bronze
Blandin Foundation

Grey Eagle

Jensen, Larry, b1954
Eagles, 1985
5'
106 State Street
wood, chainsaw
P. L. Nohner Realty Company

Hackensack

Schroeder, Doad
Lucette Diana Kensack, 1952
17'
East shore of Birch Lake
wood, cement, plaster
Artist

Ham Lake

Creative Displays
Repairman (m1987)
20'
Midstate Auto Mall, 16326 Highway 65
fiberglass
Midstate Auto Mall

Hastings

Roghair, Dennis, b1953
Eagle, 1990
7'
Veterans Administration Hospital, Chittum Park
white pine, chainsaw
Veterans Administration

Roghair, Dennis, b1953
Soldier, 1990
7'
Veterans Administration Hospital, Chittum Park
white pine, chainsaw
Veterans Administration

Hibbing

Mitchell, Robert C.
Frank Hibbing, 1941
7'
Frank Hibbing Memorial Park
bronze
WPA, city

Hill City

F.A.S.T. Corp.
Bear, 1985
9'
Park along Highway 169
fiberglass
Hill City Area Sportsmen's Club

Holdingford

Winkelman, Rev. Gilbert
Soldiers' Shrine, 1942
22' x 18' x 42'
Across from St. Hedwig's Church
fieldstone, concrete
St. Hedwig's Church

Hopkins

Raymond, Evelyn, b1908
St. Joseph, 1980
12' x 12'
St. Joseph's Church
Indiana limestone
St.Joseph's Church

Huot

Mose, Carl C., 1903–1973
Chippewa Brave, 1933
6'
Old Crossing Treaty State Park
bronze
United States Government

Hutchinson

Johnson, Robert, b1922 [see Kouba, Les]
Chief Little Crow, 1982
6'
Eheim Park
bronze
Mr. and Mrs. Les Kouba

Kouba, Les, b1917 [designer]
Chief Little Crow, 1982
6'
Eheim Park
bronze
Mr. and Mrs. Les Kouba

International Falls

Raymond, Evelyn, b1908
Sports, 1941
12' x 18'
High School Stadium, 3rd Street

concrete
WPA/ MAP

Shumaker, Gordon, b1920
Smokey the Bear, 1954
26'
Park, 3rd Street and 6th Avenue
fiberglass
Keep Minnesota Green

Lake City

Artist Unknown
Louis McCahill Memorial, 1921
6'
Highway 61 at Dwelle Street
bronze, granite
Mary McCahill

Becker, Jack
Wave, 1972
10'
Park Street near East Walnut Street
stainless steel
City, Chamber of Commerce, Regional Arts
    Council

Lake Elmo

Weimar, Dennis, b1951
Christ, 1991
12'
St. John's Lutheran Church
wood, chainsaw
Church

Lansing

Artist Unknown
Henry Bagley Monument, 1906
10'
Udolpho Cemetery
granite
Bagley family

Le Sueur

Granlund, Paul, b1925
The Mothers, 1978
65"
William Mayo House
bronze
Citizens of Le Sueur

Lilydale

Artist unknown
Indian Scout, c1900

6'
Pool and Yacht Club, Highway 13
zinc alloy, painted
J. L. Shiely

Lindstrom

Davis, Roger
The Emigrants, 1965, m1970
8' 6"
Chisago County Press, Highway 8
fiberglass
Willard Smith

Litchfield

Mullins Company, W. H.
Soldiers and Sailors Memorial, 1909
6'
Litchfield Cemetery, Sibley Avenue South
bronze, gilded
Mrs. J. M. Howard and Frank Daggett Post,
    G.A.R.

Little Falls

Jensen, L. A. "Tad"
Arvid Christopherson, 1979
7'
Lindbergh Elementary School
Ferro cement
Christopherson Memorial Committee

Littlefork

Boquist, Terry
Jackpine Savage
14'
Park, Main and 4th Street
wood, chainsaw, paint
Lions Club

Long Prairie

Daniels, John Karl, 1875–1978
World War I Memorial, 1920
7'
Todd County Court House
bronze, granite
William E. Lee

Madison

F.A.S.T. Corp.
Lou T. Fisk [codfish], 1983
L 25'
Jacobson Park
fiberglass

Madison Chamber of Commerce

Hanson, Scott
Lou T. Fisk, 1991
4′
Highway 75 North
wood, chainsaw
Madison Chamber of Commerce

Mankato

Eldred, Dale, b1934
Mankato Piece, 1968, [m1982]
40′
Pike Street Park Ramp
Cor-ten steel
Brett's, 1st National Bank

Granlund, Paul, b1925
Crucifixion [Christ and Two Thieves], 1964
5′
Bethlehem Lutheran Church
bronze
Church

Gruter, Arnold J., b1930
Waves, 1969
10′ x 12′ x 3′ 6″ deep
Mankato State University Campus
rolled steel, painted
Mrs. Doris Berger

Gruter, Arnold J., b1930
Chthonic Sculpture, 1972
7′
Mankato State University Campus
cast polyurethane, painted
n.a.

Miller, Thomas Meagher, b1961
Winter Warrior, 1987
13′
Minnesota Valley Regional Library
Kasota limestone
Dakota Indian Statue Committee and others

Miller, Thomas Meagher, b1961
Blue Earth and Nicollet Counties Vietnam
    Memorial, 1988
4′ x 4′ x 5′
Rasmussen Woods Nature Area, Stoltzman Road
Kasota limestone
MSAB

Nielsen, Stuart, b1947
River Garden, 1991
40′
Mankato Technical College

Kasota limestone
MSAB, Art in Public Places

Rudberg, Harry
Orange Cubes, 1968?
6′ x 6′
Mankato Mall near Cherry Street
steel
Artist

Maplewood

Terry, Glenn Robert
Lady Portia, Goddess of Justice, 1988
5′ 8″
Maple Hills Office Center
bronze
Maple Hills Office Center

Marshall

Peterson Company, P. N.
Soldiers and Sailors Memorial, 1911
15′
Lyon County Court House
granite
Markham Post 7, G.A.R. and Hooker Post,
    G.A.R.

Sculptured Advertising
Happy Chef
20′
Happy Chef Restaurant, Highway 19
fiberglass
Happy Chef Restaurant

Marysville

Wattenhofer, Ray, b1948
I Find No Guilt, 1983, m1991
8′ x 8′ 6″ diameter
Dyer Powell farm
bronze
Dyer Powell, owner

McIntosh

Konikson, Ernie, 1907–1977
Walking Lion, 1960
5′
Roholt Park, North of Highway 2
concrete, paint
Lions Club

Menahga

F.A.S.T. Corporation
St. Urho, 1988

12′
Helsinki Boulevard and Highway 71
fiberglass (after chainsaw original)
Menahga Civic and Commerce Association

Mendota Heights

Livia, H.
Monument to Masonry
16′ square
Acacia Park Cemetery, Pilot Knob Road
granite
Minnesota Masonic Lodges

Milaca

Roghair, Dennis, b1953
Kenny and Marilyn Trimble, 1991
6′ each
Milaca Golf Club
white pine, chainsaw
Local committee

Roghair, Dennis, b1953
Abe, 1986
6′
355 North Central
white pine, chainsaw
Pastor Hanks

Roghair, Dennis, b1953
Statue of Liberty, 1986
7′
North 4th Street and North Central Avenue
white pine, chainsaw
Milaca Centennial Committee

Roghair, Dennis, b1953
Man with Children, 1986
12′
Trimble Park
white pine, chainsaw
Milaca Centennial Committee

Sabean, Samuel, b1902
Lunette, 1936
3′ x 4′
Library (old town hall), 145 Central Avenue
    South
cast stone
WPA/ MAP

Milan

Olson, Wendell "Butch", b1931
Viking and Gnomes, 1990
11′
Main Street near library

elm, chainsaw
Chamber of Commerce

Minneapolis

Aiken, Ta-Coumba, b1953 and Jones, Seitu,
    b1951
Shadows of Spirit, 1992
various
Nicollet Mall
cast iron
Nicollet Mall Implementation Board

Akagawa, Kinji, b1940
Garden Seating, Reading, Thinking, 1987
various
Minneapolis Sculpture Garden
granite, basalt, cedar
Anonymous donor

Akagawa, Kinji, b1940
Seating Sculpture Plaza, 1992
various
Nicollet Mall, opposite Public Library
granite, wood, brass, copper
Nicollet Mall Implementation Board

Allison, Dean Kermit
The Entrepreneur, 1988
6′
Marquette Avenue at South 5th Street
bronze
University of St. Thomas

Armajani, Siah, b1939
Skyway, 1988
n.a.
Norwest Center
glass, metal
Norwest Bank

Armajani, Siah, b1939
Humphrey Institute Plaza, 1987
various
West Bank, University of Minnesota
wood, stone, metal
University of Minnesota

Armajani, Siah, b1939
Irene Hixon Whitney Bridge, 1988
L 375′
Minneapolis Sculpture Garden to Loring Park
steel, wood
Minneapolis Foundation, Whitney family,
    Mn.DOT, City of Minneapolis

Artist Unknown
St. John the Baptist de la Salle, 1941

5′
De La Salle High School
concrete
Classes of 1951 and 1952

Artist Unknown
Heffelfinger Fountain, 16th century, 1947
6′
Minneapolis Rose Gardens
marble, bronze
Frank Totton Heffelfinger

Artist Unknown
Eagle Columns, 1927, m1990
97″ x 47″ x 34″
Convention Center Walkway
Bedford granite
City of Minneapolis

Artist Unknown
Lion Dogs, c1930
H 2′ 7″ x L 1′ 10″
Hosmer Library, 347 East 36th Street
stone
Lewis S. Gillette

Artist Unknown
Firefighters Memorial, 1892
30′
Lakewood Cemetery
granite
Board of Fire Commissioners

Artists, various
Manhole Covers, 1981, 1984
21 ¾″ diameter each
Sidewalks between Nicollet, Hennepin, 6th and
    7th Streets
cast brass
Oxford Properties

Bachman, Max, 1862–1921
Abraham Lincoln [head only], 1930
13′
44th and Xerxes Avenue North
bronze
Minneapolis G.A.R. posts

Bacig, Karen Sontag, b1939
River Goddess, 1988
8′ x 84′ x 4′
West River Road near Hennepin Avenue bridge
limestone, gravel, sandstone
MSAB

Backlund, Erik Arvid, b1895
Selma Lagerlof, 1954
8′

American Swedish Institute
bronze
Major Suante Pahlson

Baizerman, Saul, 1889–1957
Nike, 1949–1952
66″
Minneapolis Sculpture Garden
copper, hammered
T. B. Walker Foundation

Barlach, Ernst, 1870–1938
The Fighter of the Spirit, 1928
12′ 2″
Main entrance, Minneapolis Institute of Arts
bronze
The John R. Van Derlip Fund

Becker, Jack
Fountain, 1978
10′
Dayton's Home Store, France Avenue and
    Gallagher Drive
stainless steel
Dayton-Hudson Corporation

Birkerts, Gunnar, b1925
Hugh Galuska Memorial Fountain, 1973
n.a.
Federal Reserve Bank plaza
Minnesota granite
Federal Reserve Bank

Bitter, Karl Theodore, 1867–1915
Thomas Lowry, 1915, m1967
8′
Emerson Avenue, 24th Street, and Hennepin
    Avenue
bronze, marble
Thomas Lowry Memorial Association

Bourgeois, Louise, b1911
The Blind Leading the Blind, 1989
88″ x 65¼″ x 16¼″
Minneapolis Sculpture Garden
bronze, paint, lacquer
Marbrook Foundation and others

Brioschi, Charles, 1879–1941, and others
Governor Floyd B. Olson, 1940
8′
Olson Highway
bronze
Olson Memorial Committee

Brodin, Rodger M., b1940
The Price of Freedom is Visible Here, 1987
5′ 6″

Veterans Administration Hospital
bronze
n.a.

Brodin, Rodger M., b1940
The Lumberman, 1990
6' 6"
Webber Park, Camden
bronze
Minneapolis Arts Commission, Celebrate
    Minnesota 1990 and others

Brodin, Rodger M., b1940
Hubert H. Humphrey, 1989
6'
City Hall
bronze
Minneapolis Arts Commission

Burke, Kate
Manhole Cover Art, 1992
22" diameter each
Nicollet Mall sidewalk
cast iron
Nicollet Mall Implementation Board

Burton, Scott, 1939–1989
Seat Legged Table, 1987, [m1992]
28" x 56" x 56"
Minneapolis Sculpture Garden
sandstone
Honeywell, Inc., in honor of Harriet and Edson
    Spencer

Butterfield, Deborah, b1949
Woodrow, 1988
99" x 105" x 74"
Minneapolis Sculpture Garden
bronze
Harriet and Edson Spencer

Calder, Alexander, 1898–1976
The Spinner, 1965
235" x 351"
Walker Art Center Terrace
aluminum, steel, oil paint
Dayton-Hudson Corporation

Caponi, Anthony, b1921
Christ, 1978
24'
Normandale Lutheran Church
copper, hammered
Church

Caponi, Anthony, b1921
Boulders on Boulders, 1982
10'
Harmon Avenue at 12th Street

Mankato limestone
Thomas Massey

Carlson, Steve, and others
Triple Totem Poles, 1975
30'
Park, opposite Nicollet Island Inn
cedar
Viking Chapter, National Woodcarvers
    Association

Caro, Anthony, b1924
Straight Flush, 1972
78" x 145" x 52"
Minneapolis Sculpture Garden
steel, paint
Judy and Kenneth Dayton

Carpenter, Bryan
Bus Top, 1988, m1991
9" x 53" x 347"
Lake Street and Thomas Avenue
steel, paint
Minneapolis Arts Commission

Chia, Sandro, b1946
Bacchus, 1988
10' 6"
Highway 12 at Highway 100
bronze
Trammell Crow-Colonnade

Cragg, Tony, b1949
Ordovician Pore, 1989
96" x 90" x 124"
Minneapolis Sculpture Garden
granite, steel
Joanne and Philip Von Blon

Cullen, Barry, b1907
[Thirty gargoyle heads], ca. 1930s
2' each
All Saints Church, 435 N. E. 4th Street
concrete
Church

Cullen, Barry, b1907
Two bas reliefs, 1939
various
Uptown Theater, 2906 Hennepin Avenue
concrete
Uptown Theater

Daniels, John Karl, 1875–1978
Pioneers, 1936, [m1967]
10' 1" x 4' x 9'
603 S. E. 5th Street
granite
City of Minneapolis

Daniels, John Karl, 1875–1978
Washburn Water Tower [Guardians and Eagles],
    1932
16' (guardians) and 8' (eagles)
Harriet and Minnehaha Avenues
stone
City of Minneapolis

Daniels, John Karl, 1875–1978
Gateway Flagstaff [Washington relief], 1917
    [recast 1966]
100'
Hennepin Avenue at 1st Street
bronze, granite
D.A.R. Monument Chapter

Daniels, John Karl, 1875–1978
Buffalo, 1948
8'
1750 Hennepin Avenue
granite
North American Life and Casualty Company

Daniels, John Karl, 1875–1978
Blacksmith and School Boy, 1923
7'
Dunwoody Institute entrance
Winona stone
Dunwoody Institute

Daniels, John Karl, 1875–1978
History of Milling, 1914
7' each (three figures)
Gold Medal Flour Building
terra cotta
General Mills

Di Suvero, Mark, b1933
Molecule, 1977, [m1991]
720"
Minneapolis Sculpture Garden
steel
Honeywell, Inc.

Di Suvero, Mark, b1933
Arikidea, 1977–1982
316" x 510" x 450"
Minneapolis Sculpture Garden
Cor-ten steel, steel, cedar
Judy and Kenneth Dayton

Di Suvero, Mark, b1933
Inner Search, 1980
30'
Norwest Gateway Square
steel
Norwest Bank

Doseff, Ivan

Six Medallions, 1948
5' diameter each
Star Tribune Building
stone
Minneapolis *Star Tribune*

Effrem, Chris, b1925
Christ, 1991
8'
St. Mary's Greek Orthodox Church, 35th Street
and Irving Avenue
wood, chainsaw
Church

Eldh, Carl Johan, 1873–1954
Gunnar Wennerberg, 1915
7'
Minnehaha Park
bronze
Wennerberg Memorial Association

Erickson, Russell, b1950
Family, 1978
various
U. S. Food and Drug Administration Building
steel rods
Samuel Marfield

Ferrara, Jackie, b1929
Belvedere, 1988
126" x 506" x 407"
Minneapolis Sculpture Garden
cedar
Butler Family Foundation

Ferrara, Jackie, b1929
A 193 Epistyle, 1978
11' x 13'
Minneapolis College of Art and Design
milled cedar
NEA grant

Fjelde, Jakob H., 1859–1896
Twenty-Four Spandrels, 1894
various
Burton Hall, University of Minnesota
stone
University of Minnesota

Fjelde, Jakob H., 1859–1896
Ole Bull, 1897
8'
Loring Park
bronze
Norwegian-American Committee

Fjelde, Jakob H., 1859–1896
Hiawatha and Minnehaha, [1893], cast 1912
8'

Minnehaha Park near Minnehaha Falls
bronze
School children of Minnesota

Fjelde, Jakob H., 1859–1896 [see Gelert, J. S.]
Colonel John H. Stevens [head only], 1912,
m1935
6' 7"
Minnehaha Park near Stevens House
bronze on granite
Mrs. Phillip Winton

Flanagan, Barry, b1941
Hare on Bell on Portland Stone Piers, 1983
102" x 112" x 75"
Minneapolis Sculpture Garden
bronze, limestone
Marilyn and Glen Nelson

Fontana, Lucio, 1899–1968
Concetto Spaziale Natura, 1961
33" x 38" x 34"
Minneapolis Sculpture Garden
bronze
T. B. Walker Foundation

Freeman, Douglas, b1953
Aurora, 1987
8' 5"
1314 Marquette Avenue
bronze
Marquette Place

Freeman, Douglas, b1953
The Family, 1989
various
150 5th Street
bronze
Opus Corporation

French, Daniel Chester, 1850–1931
Governor John Pillsbury, 1900
5'
University of Minnesota, opposite Burton Hall
bronze
Pillsbury Memorial Committee

Gehry, Frank, b1929
Standing Glass Fish, 1986
264" x 168" x 102"
Minneapolis Sculpture Garden
wood, glass, steel, silicone
Anne Pierce Rogers

Gelert, Johannes Sophus, 1852–1923 [with
Fjelde]
John H. Stevens, 1912
6' 7"
Minnehaha Park

bronze
Mrs. Phillip B. Winton

Gewoni, A. A.
H. W. Longfellow, 1908
7'
Hiawatha Avenue near 42nd Avenue South
limestone
R. F. "Fish" Jones

Ginnever, Charles, b1931
Nautilus, 1976
132" x 264" x 408"
Minneapolis Sculpture Garden
Cor-ten steel
NEA, WAC, other donors

Granlund, Paul, b1925
Twelve Credo Door Panels, 1967
18" square
Church of the Good Shepherd, France and West
48th Street
bronze
Church

Granlund, Paul, b1925
The Time Being, 1973
12'
Federal Reserve Bank Plaza, Nicollet Mall and
3rd Street
bronze, granite
Federal Reserve Bank

Granlund, Paul, b1925
Wellspring, 1985
12'
Abbott Northwestern Hospital
bronze
Hospital

Granlund, Paul, b1925
Birth of Freedom, 1976
18'
Westminster Presbyterian Church
bronze
Church

Grazzi, Peter
St. Sharbel Makhlouf, 1981
6'
St. Maron Maronite Church, 6th Street N. E. at
University Avenue
bronze
Farhet and Resha families

Hadzi, Dimitri, b1921
Arcturus, 1973
25'

Federal Reserve Plaza, Nicollet Mall and 3rd
   Street
bronze
Federal Reserve Bank

Harvey, Eli, 1860–1957
Elk, [1906], 1917
9′ 6″ x 7′ 6″
Lakewood Cemetery, Elks Rest
bronze
Elks

Hatcher, Brower, b1942
Prophecy of the Ancients, 1988
202″ x 246″
Minneapolis Sculpture Garden
cast stone, steel, bronze, aluminum
Lilly Family

Hawk, Leslie, b1953
Oasis, 1988
6′ 6″ x 9′ 7″ x 2′ 3″
7th Street at Hennepin
wood, iron, concrete
MAC, Art in Public Places

Highstein, Jene, b1942
Untitled, 1987–1988
various
Minneapolis Sculpture Garden
granite
Various donors, NEA

Holen, Norman D., b1937
Burning Bush 3, 1989
12′
Augsburg College, 731 21st Avenue South
stainless steel
Anonymous donor

Houdon, Jean Antoine, 1741–1828
George Washington, 1785–96 [cast 1931]
6′
Fair Oaks Park
bronze, granite
Minneapolis Chapter, D.A.R.

Huntington, Charles, b1925
Ojo de Dios, 1975
10″ x 10″ x 8″
1315 East 24th Street
welded steel, stainless steel
Minnesota State Arts Board

Jirka, Brad, b1954
Riverboat, 1982
9′
Riverplace over Hennepin Avenue

neon tubes
Minneapolis Parks Centennial Committee

Johnson, Daniel L.
Freedom Form No. 2, 1970
7′ x 20′ (for each piece)
King Park, 41st and Nicollet Avenue South
bronze
Artist

Jones, Seitu, b1951
Tranquility Rise, 1989
various
North Commons Park, 1801 James Avenue
   North
ceramic tile and wood
MAC, Art in Public Places

Kelly, Ellsworth, b1923
Double Curve, 1988
216″ x 40″ x4″
Minneapolis Sculpture Garden
bronze
Judy and Kenneth Dayton

Kirchner, Louis R., 1882–1958 [see Brioschi, C.]
Floyd B. Olson, 1940
8′
Olson Memorial Highway and Penn Avenue
   North
bronze
Olson Memorial Committee

Kolbe, Georg, 1877–1947
Young Woman, 1926
50″ x 14″ x 12″
Minneapolis Sculpture Garden
bronze
T. B. Walker Foundation

Landes, Harry
24 Elements, 1970–1978
33′
Honeywell Parking Area
Cor-ten steel
Honeywell, Inc.

Larson, Philip, b1944
Art Glass for Eight Transit Shelters, 1991
9′
Nicollet Mall
glass
Nicollet Mall Implementation Board

Larson, Philip, b1944
The Six Crystals, 1988
18″ x 104″ x 28″
Minneapolis Sculpture Garden

granite, cast iron
Becky and Michael Paparella

Le Witt, Sol, b1928
Three x Four x Three, 1984
169″ x 169″ x 169″
Walker Art Center Terrace
white enamel on aluminum
WAC fund

Le Witt, Sol, b1928
Lines in Two Directions, 1988
various
Minneapolis Sculpture Garden
carnelian and granite walkway
WAC, Cold Springs Granite Company

Legeros, Nicholas, b1955
The Potter, 1991
4′
Potter's House, 632 Ontario Street S. E.
bronze
Children's Transplant Association

Liberman, Alexander, b1912
Prometheus, 1964
20′ x 20′
Anderson Hall, University of Minnesota
aluminum, painted
Artist

Lichtenstein, Roy, b1923
Salute to Painting, 1985–1986
300″
Walker Art Center entrance
bronze, paint
In honor of Martin Friedman

Lindstrom, Marilyn, b1952
Neighborhood Safe Art Spot, 1991
various
Lot, 12th Avenue at Lake Street
wood, painted, mixed media
MAC

Lipchitz, Jacques, 1891–1973
Prometheus Strangling the Vulture II, 1944 [cast
   1953]
8′ 6″
Minneapolis Sculpture Garden
bronze
T. B. Walker Foundation

Luckman, Stewart
Rokker V, 1981
16′ x l26′
Williamson Hall, University of Minnesota
tubular stainless steel
University of Minnesota Alumni Association

Manzu, Giacomo, 1908–1991
La Grande Chiave, 1959
96″ x 36″ x 14″
Minneapolis Sculpture Garden
bronze
Anonymous gift

Marini, Marino, 1901–1980
Cavaliere, 1949
70″ x 45″ x 32″
Minneapolis Sculpture Garden
bronze
T. B. Walker Foundation

McAloon, Robert
Wedge, 1979
17′
Hennepin Avenue at Franklin
bronze, paint
Artist

McEachran, Marcia, b1947
Spirit, 1981
12′
Seward Square, 2121 South 9th Street
stainless steel
n.a.

McRoberts, Sheryl
Artstop, 1991
8′
Park, Chicago Avenue at 32nd Street
ceramic on wood
Minneapolis Arts Commision

Moore, Henry, 1898–1986
Standing Figure: Knife Edge, 1961
111″ x 45″ x 24″
Minneapolis Sculpture Garden
bronze
Dayton's

Moore, Henry, 1898–1986
Reclining Mother and Child, 1960–1961
90″ x 35″ x 52″
Minneapolis Sculpture Garden
bronze
T. B. Walker Foundation

Morrison, George, b1919
Tableau: A Native American Mosaic, 1992
22′ x 36′
Nicollet Mall at IDS Center
granite mosaics
Nicollet Mall Implementation Board

Morrison, George, b1919
Feather Motif, 1975
18′ x 96′

American Indian Center, Franklin Avenue
wood inlays
NEA grant

Mosman, Warren, (designer) 1909–1968
Farmer and Mechanic, [reliefs] 1941
n.a.
Marquette Bank Building, 88 South 6th Street
n.a.
Farmers and Mechanics Bank

Murray, Robert, b1936
Taku, 1979
30′ wide
Honeywell Plaza
Cor-ten steel
Honeywell, Inc.

Nagare, Masayuki
[Untitled], 1965
various
Northwestern National Life Insurance Co.
marble
Northwestern National Life Insurance Company

Nakian, Reuben, b1897
Goddess with the Golden Thighs, 1964–1965
[cast 1987]
84″ x 150″ x 42″
Minneapolis Sculpture Garden
bronze
Dolly J. Fiterman

Nash, David, b1945
Standing Frame, 1987
172″ x 209″ x 209″
Minneapolis Sculpture Garden
white oak
Star Tribune and Cowles Media Foundation

Nelson, Jack
Sculpture Clock, 1967
12′
Nicollet Mall at 9th Street
metal, steel, glass
Nicollet Mall Implementation Board

Nesjar, Carl, b1920
Ice/ Water Fountain, 1991
12′
Nicollet Mall between 5th and 6th Streets
stainless steel, granite
Nicollet Mall Implementation Board

Noguchi, Isamu, 1904–1988
Shodo Shima, 1978
12″ x 66″ x 69″ overall
Minneapolis Sculpture Garden

granite
Artist

Noguchi, Isamu, 1904–1988
Theatre Set for "Judith", 1950, [cast 1978]
108″ x 109″ x 54″
Minneapolis Sculpture Garden
bronze
WAC, NEA, and other donors

Offner, Elliot, b1931
Sculpture Fountain, 1992
11′ x 15′ x 9′
Nicollet Mall south of 9th Street
bronze, granite
Nicollet Mall Implementation Board

Oldenburg, Claes, b1929
Geometric Mouse - Scale A, 1974
145″ x 143″ x 73″
Walker Art Center terrace
steel, aluminum, paint
WAC

Oldenburg, Claes, b1929 and van Bruggen,
  Coosje
Spoonbridge and Cherry, 1987–1988
354″ x 618″ x 162″
Minneapolis Sculpture Garden
stainless steel, painted aluminum
Frederick R. Weisman

Perkins and Kratzert Company
Soldiers' Monument, 1923
11′ 8″ x 18′ x 6′ 6″
Lakewood cemetery
Minnesota white granite, bronze
Soldiers' Monument Association

Perry, Charles, b1929
Thrice, 1973
20′ x 17′
Federal Reserve Plaza
stainless steel, painted
Federal Reserve Bank

Prokopiof, Bill, b1944
Cold Wind Walk, 1989
4′
Nicollet Center, 514 Nicollet Mall
welded steel
Edward Baker

Puryear, Martin, b1941
Ampersand, 1987–1988
163″ (east column) and 167″ (west column)
Minneapolis Sculpture Garden
Cold Spring granite
Margaret and Angus Wurtele

Rapson, Ralph, b1914
Riverside Plaza, 1968
various
Cedar Square West
steel, concrete
Cedar-Riverside Associates

Raymond, Evelyn, b1908
Legacy, 1982
14'
Courtyard entrance, Fairview Riverside Hospital
bronze, gilded
Fairview Hospital 75th Anniversary Committee

Raymond, Evelyn, b1908
St. Augustine of Hippo, 1963
12'
Church of St. Austin, 41st and Thomas Avenue
    North
copper
Church of St. Austin

Raymond, Evelyn, b1908
Shepherd Boy, 1950
16'
Church of the Good Shepherd, facade
stone
Church of the Good Shepherd

Rood, John, 1902–1974
The Scroll, 1960
27' x 22'
Minneapolis Public Library, Nicollet Mall
steel, copper plates
Private donors and Dorothy B. Atkinson Rood

Rood, John, 1902–1974
Don Quixote, 1960
6' 11" x 3' 10" x 3'
Law School, University of Minnesota
bronze
Mr. and Mrs. Julius Davis

Rose, Tom, b1942
Chippendale Couch, 1988
3' 2" x 6' 11" x 1' 8"
Public Library near Hennepin Avenue
cast iron and paint
Minneapolis Arts Commission

Roszak, Theodore, b1907
Cradle Song Variation No. 2, 1959–1960
65" x 21" x 36"
Minneapolis Sculpture Garden
steel brazed with bronze
T. B. Walker Foundation

Ruggles-Kitson, Theo Alice, 1872–1932
Spanish American War Soldier, 1906

6'
Armory, University of Minnesota
bronze
Alumni and Friends of University students

Saint-Gaudens, Augustus, 1848–1907
Abraham Lincoln [replica of body], [1887], 1929
7'
G.A.R. Circle, Victory Memorial Drive
bronze
Minneapolis units of G.A.R.

Sears, Stanton, b1950
Two Boatlike Seating Sculptures, 1992
L 14'
Nicollet Mall
granite
Nicollet Mall Implementation Board

Sears, Stanton, b1950
Water Toy Bench, 1988
various
Hennepin Avenue between 7th and 8th
bronze
Minneapolis Arts Commission

Segal, George, b1924
Walking Man, 1988
72" x 36" x 30"
Minneapolis Sculpture Garden
bronze
A.T.& T. Foundation and Julius Davis family

Serra, Richard, b1939
Five Plates, Two Poles, 1971
96" x 276" x 216"
Minneapolis Sculpture Garden
Cor-ten steel
Judy and Kenneth Dayton

Severson, William, b1924, and Schultz,
    Saunders, b1927
Tetraedros Sculpture, 1986
10'
IDS Center at Nicollet Mall
stainless steel
IDS

Shea, Judith, b1948
Without Words, 1988
78" x 80" x 118"
Minneapolis Sculpture Garden
bronze, cast marble, limestone
Jeanne and Richard Levitt

Silver, Jonathan, b1937
Wounded Amazon, 1982–1983
85" x 21" x 16"
Minneapolis Sculpture Garden

bronze
Sidney Singer

Slifer, Fred A.
Father Louis Hennepin, 1930
29'
Hennepin Avenue at 16th Street
copper
Knights of Columbus

Smith, Tony, 1912–1980
Amaryllis, 1965, [constructed 1968]
134" x 108" x 144"
Minneapolis Sculpture Garden
Cor-ten steel, paint
T. B. Walker Foundation

Snelson, Kenneth, b1927
Northwood III, 1982
12' x 12' x 30'
Honeywell Park
stainless steel, pipe, cable
Honeywell, Inc.

Sosin, Georgette, b1934
The Healing Spirit, 1980, m1991
28'
Abbott-Northwestern Hospital
commercial welded bronze
Judaism and Medicine Competition

Stankiewicz, Richard, 1922–1983
Grass, 1980–1981
151" x 104" x 37"
Minneapolis Sculpture Garden
steel
Judy and Kenneth Dayton

Sullivan Monument Company, J. M.
Soldiers and Sailors Memorial, 1903
25'
Lakewood Cemetery, section 8
bronze
Minneapolis units of G.A.R.

Von Koelnau, Louis "Red", b1924
Moebius Strip, 1977
12'
Whittier Park, 26th and Grand Avenue South
fiberglass
Minneapolis Park Board, Dayton-Hudson
    Foundation, MSAB

Walker, Nellie V., 1874–1973
Woman, 1920
5' 8"
Lakewood Cemetery, section 23
bronze
McMullen family

Wells, Charles, 1873–1956
The Phelps Fountain, 1915, m1963
13′ 8″
Minneapolis Rose Gardens
marble, bronze
Edmund J. Phelps

Woodward, Robert
Berger Fountain, 1975
17′ diameter
Willow Street at Loring Park
copper tubes
Benjamin Berger

Woodward, Steven, b1953
Another Conundrum, 1988
130″ x 102″ x 374″
Minneapolis Sculpture Garden
wood, modified bitumen, steel, paint
T. B. Walker Acquisition Fund

Minnetonka

Erickson, Russell, b1950
Spirit, 1981
37′ x 25′ x 10′
Ridge Square North Shopping Center
steel rods
Samuel Marfield

Erickson, Russell, b1950
Together, 1984
25′ x 15′ diameter
Baker Technology Plaza
steel rods
Samuel Marfield

Erickson, Russell, b1950
We are just a song, 1989
10′
Rowland Pond Center, 5600–5610 Rowland
    Road
steel rods
Marfield, Belgarde and Yaffe

Erickson, Russell, b1950
Meditation, 1985
9′ diameter
Rowland Pond Center, 5600–5610 Rowland
    Road
steel rods
Marfield, Belgarde and Yaffe

Erickson, Russell, b1950
Tetra Peak of Technology, 1985
n.a.
Baker Technology Center
steel rods

Samuel Marfield

Tew, Gloria
Soaring, 1987
12′
Minnetonka Civic Center
stainless steel
City of Minnetonka

Montevideo

Blanes, Juan Manuel, 1830–1910
The Liberator [Jose Artigas], 1898, cast 1949
5′
Artigas Plaza on the Mall
bronze
Citizens of Montevideo, Uruguay

Moorhead

Fjelde, Paul, b1892
Ivar Andreas Aasen, 1913
3′
Founders Court, Concordia College
bronze on granite
Aasen Memorial Committee

Jacobson, Raymond, b1920
Arvegods, 1979
12′
Founders Court, Concordia College
copper
Clarence H. Berg

Rostad, Merlin, b1913
Squares in Symmetry, 1986
8′ 6″ x 6′ 6″ x 16′
Comstock Theater, Concordia College
aluminum castings on granite base
Artist

Moose Lake

F.A.S.T. Corp.
Moose, 1989
9′
Park on Highway 61
fiberglass
City of Moose Lake

Mora

Artist Unknown
Dala Horse, 1971
22′
Kanabec County Fairgrounds, Highway 65
fiberglass
Mora Jaycees

Mounds View

Johnson, Robert, b1922
Mermaid, 1967
30′
2200 Highway 10
fiberglass
Mermaid Supper Club

Mountain Iron

Crump, Robert, b1907
Leonidas Merritt, 1940
10′ 6″
Mountain Iron Library
cast stone
WPA/MAP

Nevis

Ballard, Warren
Tiger Muskie, 1950
L 30′ 6″
Park, Main Street
cedar and redwood
Nevis Civic and Commerce Association

New Ulm

Dingman, Gordon
Life Sketches, 1972
various
16 Minnesota Street North
fired brick
Local Committee

Pelzer, Alfonso, d1904
Hermann the Cheruscan, 1890
102′
Hermann Heights Park
sheet metal, copper, bronze, zinc
Sons of Hermann Lodges

North Mankato

Miller, Thomas Meagher, b1961
World War II Veterans Memorial, 1989
10′
Wheeler Park
Kasota limestone
Veterans Memorial Committee

North St. Paul

Koesling, Lloyd, and others
Snowman, 1974, m1990
54′
North Margaret Street and Centennial Drive

concrete stucco
North St. Paul Chamber of Commerce

Northfield

Artist Unknown
Soldiers and Sailors Memorial, 1921
12'
Bridge Square, Division and 4th Street
bronze, granite
G.A.R.

Berge, Dorothy, b1923
The Spirit Also Helpeth, 1991
n.a.
Skoglund Athletic Center, St. Olaf College
Cor-ten steel
St. Olaf College

Field, Richard
Voices, Thoughts & Spirits in the Wind, 1977,
  m1984
7'
City Hall, 9th and Washington
Cor-ten steel
MSAB and local donors

Granlund, Paul, b1925
Crucifixion, 1982
12'
St. Olaf College, Administration Building
bronze
Anonymous donor

Granlund, Paul, b1925
Community, 1982
L 28'
St. Olaf College, Administration Building
bronze
Anonymous donor

Granlund, Paul, b1925
Creation, 1982
5'
St. Olaf College, Administration Building
bronze
Anonymous donor

Granlund, Paul, b1925
Resurrection, 1982
22'
St. Olaf College, Administration Building
bronze
Anonymous donor

Hadzi, Dimitri, b1921
Carleton Arch, 1986
18'

Library, Carleton College
stone
Robert and Karen Larson

Jacobson, Raymond, b1920
Jennifer Bonner Memorial Garden, 1989
various
Boliou Hall, Carleton College
bronze, various
Jennifer Bonner Memorial Committee

Jacobson, Raymond, b1920
Anniversary Fountain, 1980
4'
Bridge Square, Division and 4th Street
bronze, steel
Sheldahl Corporation

Jacobson, Raymond, b1920
Centennial Fountain, 1967
8'
Boliou Hall, Carleton College
phosphorous copper, stainless steel
Carleton Centennial Committee

Jacobson, Raymond, b1920 (see Wells, C.)
Laudie Porter Memorial Sun Dial, 1991
2'
Laird Hall, Carleton College
bronze
Laudie Porter Memorial Committee

Mojsilov, Zoran, b1955
Bashchelik, 1987
12'
near Manitou Hall, St. Olaf College
wood, rope
St. Olaf College

Nygaard, Kaare, 1903–1989
Cancer I, 1959
25'x 10' x 7' 5"
Entrance, St. Olaf College
bronze
Bequest of artist

Slawson, David
Japanese Peace Garden, 1974
various
Carleton College
various media
Carleton College

Wells, Charles, 1873–1956
Anna T. Lincoln Sun Dial, 1921
3'
Laird Hall, Carleton College
granite base (sundial replaced)

Lincoln Memorial Committee

Zelenak, Ed, b1941
People Pocket, 1972
various
Carleton College, between Chapel and Art
  Gallery
wood, stone, earth
Carleton College

Olivia

Dallas Displays
Ear of Corn, 1973
25'
Memorial Park, Highway 212
fiberglass
Olivia Chamber of Commerce

Onamia

Roghair, Dennis, b1953
Sheriff, 1985
5'
First State Bank, Main Street
white pine, chainsaw
First State Bank

Roghair, Dennis, b1953
Fresh Meat Man, 1985
5'
Hills Grocery, Main Street
white pine, chainsaw
Hills Grocery

Orono

Legeros, Nicholas, b1955
Birdbath, 1988
3' x 2' 6"
Livingston Tower Park
bronze
City of Orono

Oronoco

Gage, John, b1951
Gold Miner, 1989
12'
Main Street
elm, chainsaw
City of Oronoco

Orr

Shumaker, Gordon, b1920
Bluegill
5' x 10'

Highway 53, south of city
fiberglass
Orr Chamber of Commerce

Ortonville

Artist Unknown
Paul Bunyan's Anchor, 1958
n.a.
Highway 12 west of Highway 75
granite
Ortonville Centennial Committee

Garatti, John B., 1881–1949
War Memorial, 1920
12′
Court House, 2nd Street S. E. and Lincoln
   Avenue
granite
Ortonville Memorial Committee

Mullins Company, W. H.
Soldiers and Sailors Memorial, 1914
6′
Mound Cemetery, Stevens Street
bronze
Frank Blair Post 82, G.A.R. and WRC Post 20

Osakis

Jensen, Larry, b1954
Indian, 1988
8′
6th Avenue and Lake Street
elm, chainsaw, paint
Chamber of Commerce

Owatonna

Artist Unknown
Mercy, Justice and Law, 1892
8′
Steele County Court House
metal, paint
Steele County

Berghs, Larry and William
Princess Owatonna, [1931], m1986
6′
Mineral Springs Park
concrete
City of Owatonna

Gagnon, Charles E., b1934
Spirit of Peace, 1973
8′
Art Center Sculpture Garden
bronze

Owatonna Arts Center

Granlund, Paul, b1925
Reflections, 1979
5′ 8″
Art Center Sculpture Garden
bronze
Owatonna Art Center

Jensen, Jon
Theatre Set for "A Midsummer Night's Dream",
   1972
15′
Owatonna Art Center
steel rods, metal screening
Guthrie Theatre

Rood, John, 1902–1974
Winged Figure, 1953
4′
Arts Center Sculpture Garden
bronze
Owatonna Art Center

Park Rapids

Creative Displays
Leaping Stag, 1977
L 20′
"Deertown", Highway 71
fiberglass
Deertown

Pelican Rapids

Resset, T., Resset, A., and Anderson, Alan
Pelican, 1957
15′ 6″
Mill Pond Dam
concrete
Pelican Rapids Chamber of Commerce

Pequot Lakes

Jensen, Larry, b1954
Indian, 1987
28′
Information Center
wood, chainsaw, paint
Chamber of Commerce

Pipestone

Artist Unknown
Justice, 1900
8′
Pipestone County Court House
bronze

Pipestone County

Moore, Leon H., 1844–1907
Seventeen Relief Heads, 1896
various
102 Main Street E. at Hiawatha (Moore Block)
Sioux quartzite
Artist

Moore, Leon H., 1844–1907
Soldiers and Sailors Memorial, 1901
6′ 2″
Court House Square
granite
Pipestone Soldier's Monument Committee

Preston

F.A.S.T. Corp.
Trout, 1988
L 19′
Park on Highway 52
fiberglass
Preston Commercial Club

Pinske, Barry, b1963
Trout, 1987
6′
City Hall
wood, chainsaw
Preston Commercial Club

Ray

Beyers, Duane
Lake Kabetogama Walleye, 1949
16′
Highway 53 and County Road No. 122
concrete
Lake Kabetogama Lake Association

Red Wing

Artist Unknown
Bay Point Park Memorial, 1984
various
Bay Point Park
metal poles, limestone
Red Wing Preservation Commission and others

Artist Unknown
Soldiers and Sailors Memorial, 1913
22′
Goodhue County Court House
granite
Soldier's Monument Association

Artist Unknown

Firefighters Memorial, 1900
20'
Oakwood Cemetery, East Avenue at 16th Street
granite
Board of Fire Commissioners

Remer

F.A.S.T. Corp.
Eagle, 1983
11' 6"
Main Street
fiberglass
City of Remer

Rochester

Crunelle, Leonard, 1872–1944
W. W. Mayo, 1911
10'
Mayo Park
bronze
Mayo Memorial Committee

Fraser, James Earle, 1876–1953
Dr. William and Dr. Charles Mayo, 1952
10'
Civic Center
bronze
Mayo Memorial Committee

Gagnon, Charles E., b1934
St. Francis and the Birds, 1969
10'
St. Mary's Hospital
bronze
St. Mary's Hospital

Gagnon, Charles E., b1934
The Peace Fountain, 1989
10'
Peace Plaza
bronze
Rochester Peace Fountain Committee

Hepworth, Barbara, 1903–1975
Four-Square (walk through), 1960–1969
15'
Harwick Building, Mayo Clinic
bronze
Constantine P. Goulandris Family

Hoffman, Malvina, 1885–1966
St. Francis and the Wolf, 1966
4'
St. Mary's Hospital
bronze
Charles Hoffman

Huntington, Charles, b1925
Untitled, 1989
18' x 7' x 7'
Mayo Park, East Center Street
welded steel, stainless steel
City of Rochester

Huntington, Charles, b1925
Hope, 1983
10' x 3' x 3'
Guggenheim Building, Mayo Clinic
welded steel, stainless steel
Ronald Raimundo family

Kirchner, Louis R., 1882–1958
Eagle [on Memorial to all Wars,] 1931
13'
Soldiers Memorial Field
bronze, granite
Soldier's Memorial Committee

Kooiman, Mayo, b1931
Edith Graham Mayo, 1953
5' 6"
St. Mary's Hospital
bronze
Mayo family members

Luckman, Stewart
[untitled], 1975
various
Rochester Community College
Cor-ten steel
n.a.

Mestrovic, Ivan, 1883–1962
Man and Freedom, 1954
15'
Mayo Building, 1st Street S. W.
bronze
Mayo Clinic

Milles, Carl, 1875–1955
Shell Blowing Triton, 1916
7' 3"
Mayo Building, 1st Street S. W.
bronze on granite
Mr. and Mrs. Daniel Gainey

Pattison, Abbott, b1916
Man and Recreation, 1954
various
Mayo Building, 2nd Street S. W.
welded bronzed copper
Mayo Clinic

Wynne, David, b1926
Boy with a Dolphin, 1984
13'

Mayo Building, 2nd Street S. W.
bronze
Gift of Count Theo and Countess Ida Rossi

Zorach, William, 1887–1966
Man and Achievement [four figures], 1952–1953
various
Mayo Building, 2nd Avenue S.W.
bronze
Mayo Clinic

Roseville

Granlund, Paul, b1925
Cube Column Resurrection, 1991
12'
Roselawn Cemetery
bronze
Roselawn cemetery

Johnson, Robert, b1922
Eagle, 1958, m1987
18'
Northwestern College
fiberglass
Minnesota Federal Savings and Loan Association

Rothsay

Fosse, Art, and Western, Dale
Booming Prairie Chicken, 1976
13' x 18'
Art Fosse Park
cement
Rothsay Bicentennial Committee

Sauk Rapids

Wippich, Louis C., 1896–1973
Molehill, 1948–1973
various
601 3rd Avenue North
scrap granite
Artist

Shoreview

Ward, Jerry, b1947
Chainsaw Man
5'
Tilton Equipment Company, 4575 Chatsworth
    Street
wood, chainsaw
Tilton Equipment Company

Silver Bay

Artist Unknown
Rocky Taconite, 1964, m1990

12'
Outer Drive, east of Highway 61
plate steel on taconite rock
Silver Bay Chamber of Commerce, Reserve
    Mining Company

Sleepy Eye

Herter Company
World Record Jackalope, 1985
3'
Heiderscheid Monument Company
fiberglass
Heiderscheid Company

South St. Paul

Ogle, Philip Brandon, b1943
A Touch of Class, 1983
100' x 24' x 40'
Villaume & South Concord Streets
Cor-ten steel, cable
A Touch of Class Committee

Stillman, Bruce, b1958
Central Square Sculpture, 1980
various
South St. Paul High School
steel
MSAB, St. Paul Foundation, and Civic Arts
    Board

Zinz, Robert Lee
Minnesota - the State, 1976
4'
Municipal Building, Marie Street
bronze
Local Committee

Spring Valley

Artist Unknown
Soldiers and Sailors Memorial, 1892
15'
Spring Valley Cemetery
bronze
Burdick Post 3, G.A.R. and WRC 3

Landsverk, Halvor, b1909
Chief Decorah, c1940, m1989
12'
Tourist Information Kiosk
concrete
City of Spring Valley

St. Cloud

Brodin, Rodger M., b1940
Leaf, 1978

10'
Sunwood Inn
welded steel, paint
Sunwood Inn

Caponi, Anthony, b1921
The Granite Trio, 1973
various
Mall St. Germain
granite
MSAB, local donors

Garatti, John B., 1881–1949
James J. Hill, 1939
12'
Near Lake George
granite
Great Northern Railway Veterans Association

Huntington, Charles, b1925
Perspectives, 1990
12' x 20' x 20'
St. Cloud State College
welded stainless steel
MSAB, Art in Public Places

Marcheschi, Cork, b1945
St. Cloud Slapshot, 1990
L 70'
Ice Hockey Arena, St. Cloud State University
aluminum, steel, neon tubes
MSAB, Art in Public Places

Mastroiani, Domenico
Father Francis Xavier Pierz, 1952
12'
St. Cloud Hospital
bronze
Pierz Memorial Committee

Pelzer, Alfonso, d1904
Abraham Lincoln, [1898], cast 1918
7'
near Veterans Memorial Bridge
sheet copper
Various veterans groups

St. Paul

Arnold, Hillis, b1906
[Reliefs on Entrance Doors], 1971
8' x 3'
First Baptist Church
bronze
First Baptist Church

Arnold, Hillis, b1906
The Cross of Mercy, 1960
8'

Facade, St. Joseph's Hospital
bronze
St. Joseph's Hospital

Artist Unknown
Firefighters' Memorial, 1891
20'
Oakland Cemetery, Sycamore and Jackson
    Streets
cast iron
Board of Fire Commissioners

Artist Unknown
St. Joseph the Worker, 1944
6'
Crandell and Stanton Halls, College of St.
    Catherine
cement
Anonymous donor

Artist Unknown
Sacred Heart, 1923
12'
College of St. Catherine
Carrara marble
Alumnae Association

Artist Unknown
Schiffman Fountain, 1898
6'
Como Park
cast iron on concrete
Rudolph Schiffman

Artist Unknown
Pair of Lions, 1923–1924
H 2' 4" x L 3' 5"
Caecelian Hall, College of St. Catherine
bronze
Patrick Rahilly

Artist Unknown
Our Lady of Peace, 1944
8'
near Library, College of St. Catherine
cement
College of St. Catherine students

Artist Unknown
Firefighters Memorial, 1891
20'
Oakland Cemetery, Sycamore and Jackson
    Streets
cast iron
Board of Fire Commissioners

Artist Unknown
Bullfrog, 1923
4'

Lily pond, Como Park
granite
Gift of Fred Crosby

Bengtson, Elizabeth
Statue of Liberty, [1976], m1986
12'
MSF, Agriculture Building
wood, chainsaw
Anonymous Gift

Beyer, Steve, b1951
Untitled, 1977
5'
Douglas Park
steel
COMPAS

Beyer, Steve, b1951
Untitled, 1976
6' x 9' x 4'
Museum Park, Exchange and Cedar Streets
steel
COMPAS

Bigger, Michael, b1937
Through the Looking Glass #1
7' x 6'
Hamline Sculpture Garden
welded steel, paint
Van Landschoot Family and Hamline Midway
    Coalition

Bigger, Michael, b1937
Through the Looking Glass #3
7' x 6'
Hamline Sculpture Garden
welded steel, paint
Van Landschoot Family and Hamline Midway
    Coalition

Bigger, Michael, b1937
Waterfall #7, 1989
8' x 4'
Hamline Sculpture Garden
welded steel, paint
Van Landschoot Family and Hamline Midway
    Coalition

Bigger, Michael, b1937
Le Sorelle, 1985
10'
Hamline Sculpture Garden
welded steel, paint
Van Landschoot Family and Hamline Midway
    Coalition

Brioschi, Amerigo
Governor Floyd B. Olson, 1958

8'
Capitol Mall
bronze
State of Minnesota

Brioschi, Charles, 1879–1941
Christopher Columbus, 1931
10'
Capitol Mall
bronze
Columbus Memorial Committee

Brodin, Rodger M., b1940
Monument to the Living, 1982
12'
Capitol Mall
steel plates
VFW, Department of Minnesota

Caponi, Anthony, b1921
[untitled], 1980
10'
Macalester College
granite
Macalester College

Clarke, Geoffrey, b1924
Uniforge, 1967
L 16'
Jackson and 5th Streets
cast aluminum
Farm Credit Banks

Clarke, Geoffrey, b1924
Triuni, 1967
16'
Jackson and 5th Streets
cast aluminum
Farm Credit Banks

Contreras, Estanislao
La Nuova Vita, 1983
10'
St. Peter and 5th Street
red stone
Amhoist Tower

Corwin, Albert S., 1861–1940
Figures and Eagles, 1898–1905
8'6" each
Minnesota State Capitol
marble
State of Minnesota

Creative Displays and F.A.S.T. Corp.
Collection of Animals and Figures, 1974 to date
various
Fairway Golf Center, 1700 Como Avenue

fiberglass
Norb Anderson

Daniels, John Karl, 1875–1978
Earthbound, 1956
7'
Veterans Services Building
Vermont marble
n.a.

Daniels, John Karl, 1875–1978
Knute Nelson, 1928
9'
Capitol Mall
bronze
Nelson Memorial Committee

Daniels, John Karl, 1875–1978
Soldiers and Sailors Memorial, 1903
53'
Summit and Marshall Avenues
bronze
Acker Post 21, G.A.R.

Daniels, John Karl, 1875–1978
Leif Erikson, 1948
13'
University and Constitution Avenues
bronze
Leif Erikson Monument Association

Ed, Robert Bertil, b1920
Christ, 1981
8'
St. Anthony Park Lutheran Church, facade
redwood
Church

Erickson, Russell, b1950
Wall of Words, 1979
24' x 17' x 12'
600 Transit Blvd
steel rods
Samuel Marfield

Erickson, Russell, b1950
Fabric of the Community, 1980
17' x 14' x 8'
Amtrak Station
steel rods
Artist

Erickson, Russell, b1950
The Energy Park Sun, 1983
26'
Energy Park Business Center
steel rods
Samuel Marfield

Feehan, H. V.
Our Lady Queen of Peace, 1950
10'
University of St. Thomas
granite
University of St. Thomas students

Ferber, Herbert, 1906–1991
Let Justice Well Up, 1956
8'
Temple of Aaron, facade
wrought iron, wire
Temple of Aaron

Ferrara, Jackie, b1929
Hamm Plaza, 1991
various
Hamm Plaza
granite, stainless steel
St. Paul Companies, City of St. Paul

Fleischner, Richard, b1944
Benches, Walls, Columns, 1991
various
Minnesota Judicial Center
stone, wood
MSAB, Art in Public Places

Freeman, Douglas, b1953
Spiral of Birds, 1991
12'
Presbyterian Home, 1910 W. County Road D
bronze
Presbyterian Home

French, Daniel Chester, 1850–1931 [see Potter]
The Progress of the State [figures], 1905
various
Minnesota State Capitol
sheet metal, copper
State of Minnesota

Garatti, John B., 1881–1949
Heat, Light and Power, 1930
n.a.
Ecolab Center, 360 Wabasha
aluminum
Northern States Power Company

Garten, Cliff, b1954
Chapel Site Sculpture, 1991
various
Kellogg and Minnesota Streets
bronze, stone
City of St. Paul

Ginnever, Charles, b1931
Protagoras, 1976

10' x 30' x 14'
Federal Courts Building, Robert Street and
    Kellogg Blvd.
welded steel
GSA Art in Architecture

Granlund, Paul, b1925
Harry & Adelaide NcNeely, 1981
6'
University of St. Thomas, McNeely Hall
bronze
n.a

Granlund, Paul, b1925
Charles A. Lindbergh, Man and Boy, 1985
various
Capitol Mall
bronze
n.a.

Granlund, Paul, b1925
Man-Nam, 1970
8'
Governor's Residence, Summit Avenue
bronze
Vietnam Memorial Committee

Granlund, Paul, b1925
Zerogee, 1983
27"
College of St. Catherine
bronze
Helen & Tom Coughlan

Granlund, Paul, b1925
Bethesda Angel, 1968
66"
Bethesda Lutheran Medical Center
bronze
Bethesda Lutheran Medical Center

Granlund, Paul, b1925
Constellation Earth, 1984
7" sphere
University of St. Thomas
bronze
Virginia Coughlan

Hall, Charlie (designer)
A Tribute to Volunteers, 1987
17'
Phalen Park, west shore of lake, north of Picnic
    Pavilion
Vermont granite
Ice Palace Tribute Committee

Hauser, Alonzo, 1909–1988
The Source [Fountain], 1965

7'
Rice Park
bronze
St. Paul Women's Institute

Hauser, Alonzo, 1909–1988
Promise of Youth [fountain], 1962
various
Veterans Service Building
bronze
n.a.

Hauser, Alonzo, 1909–1988
Christ, 1952
16'
St. Paul Evangelical & Reformed Church
Bedford stone
Church

Holyoke, Thomas G., 1884–1925
World War I Memorial [Celtic Cross], 1923
36'
Summit Avenue at Mississippi River Blvd.
granite
St. Paul Chapter, D.A.R.

Hunter, John, b1950
Bride and Groom, 1988
4'
MSF, Agriculture Building, Underwood Street
elm, chainsaw
Minnesota State Fair Association

Hunter, John, b1950
Fairchild, 1983
11'
MSF Bandshell, Cosgrove Street
elm, chainsaw
Minnesota State Fair Association

Hunter, John, b1950
Clown with Accordion, 1988
6' 4"
MSF, Home Improvement, Cooper Street
elm, chainsaw
Minnesota State Fair Association

Hunter, John, b1950
Clown with Balloons, 1989
10'
MSF, Food Building, Underwood Street
elm, chainsaw
Minnesota State Fair Association

Hunter, John, b1950
Voyageur, 1990
11'
MSF, Commonwealth Avenue

elm, chainsaw
Minnesota State Fair Association

Hunter, John, b1950
Fairborne, 1985
10'
MSF, Chambers Street
elm, chainsaw
Minnesota State Fair Association

Hunter, John, b1950
Campbell Soup Chef, 1989
4' 5"
MSF, Cosgrove Street
elm, chainsaw
Minnesota State Fair Association

Hunter, John, b1950
Rooster, 1990
7'
MSF, Poultry Barn, Judson Avenue
elm, chainsaw
Minnesota State Fair Association

Hunter, John, b1950
Tumblers, 1990
10'
MSF, Commonwealth Avenue
elm, chainsaw
Minnesota State Fair Association

Johnson, Robert, b1922
Indian Hunter and his Dog, 1983 (Manship
    replica)
5' 4" x 6' 2"
Cochran Park
fiberglass
City of St. Paul

Johnson, Robert, b1922
Octopus, 1967
8'
2910 University Avenue
fiberglass
Octopus Car Wash

Jones, Seitu, b1951
Dred Scott Memorial, 1991
W 14'
Fort Snelling
concrete tiles
MHS grants-in-aid, Forecast, FMC Corporation

Kiselewski, Joseph, 1901–1988
St. Jerome, 1958
4' 8"
O'Shaughnessy Library, University of St.
    Thomas
stone

University of St. Thomas

Lawrie, Lee, 1877–1963
Relief Panels, 1931–1932
6' x 4' (each)
City Hall and County Court House, Kellogg
    Blvd.
concrete
Ramsey County, City of St. Paul

Leicester, Andrew John, b1948
Gnomon, 1985
various
Energy Park Drive
paving stones
Purop Northamerica

Liberman, Alexander, b1912
Above, Above, 1972
25' x 12'
Ecolab Center Terrace
welded steel, painted
Economics Laboratory

Lupori, Peter, b1918
St. Francis of Assisi, 1987
3'
College of St. Catherine, English Garden
bronze
Patrick and Alice S. Rogers

Manship, Paul Howard, 1885–1966
Indian Hunter and his Dog, 1926, m1967
5' 4" x 6' 2"
McKnight Formal Garden, Como Park
bronze
Thomas Cochran, Jr.

Marcheschi, Cork, b1945
Hannibal, 1985
36' x 12' x 3'
Actor's Theatre, 7th Place
neon and stucco
Actor's Theatre

McKenzie, Dr. Robert Tait, 1867–1938
Boy Scout, [1937], 1967
6'
Indianhead Boy Scout Council, 493 Marshall
    Avenue
bronze
Boy Scouts of America

Nash, Katherine, 1910–1982
Women's Day and Year, 1975
6' diameter
MSF Administration Building, Cosgrove Street
stainless steel
MSAB, General Mills Foundation, and others

Nesse, J. Paul
Frank Boyd, 1976
3'
Boyd Park, Dayton Avenue
bronze
City of St. Paul

Noguchi, Isamu, 1904–1988
Fountain, 1966
12'
Lila Wallace Court, Macalester College
welded bronze
Macalester College

Omatti, Giuseppi
Love, 1950 [Dr. Herman A. Dreschler tomb]
24'
Calvary Cemetery
granite
Dreschler family

O'Connor, Andrew J., Jr., 1874–1941
John Albert Johnson Memorial, 1912
9'
State Capitol Mall
bronze
Johnson Memorial Committee

Partridge, William Ordway, 1861–1930
Nathan Hale, 1907
7'
Summit, Western, and Portland Avenues
bronze, granite
Nathan Hale Chapter, D.A.R.

Potter, Edward, 1837–1923
The Progress of the State [horses] 1905
various
Minnesota State Capitol
sheet metal, copper
State of Minnesota

Price, Michael, b1940
Archbishop John Ireland, 1989
6' 3"
University of St. Thomas
bronze
Virginia Donahue

Price, Michael, b1940
The Olivet Triptych, 1987
3' each
Olivet Congregational Church, 1850 Iglehart
bronze
Olivet Centennial Committee

Ravinsky, Hans
The Burning Bush, 1960
6' 2"

Mount Zion Temple
bronze
Mount Zion Temple

Raymond, Evelyn, b1908
The Family, 1959, m1983
18' x 21'
Coughlan Fieldhouse, University of St. Thomas
copper, hammered
Mutual Service Insurance Company

Rickey, George b1907
Two Lines Oblique, 1967–1968
25'
Museum Park, Exchange and Cedar Streets
stainless steel
Minnesota Museum of Art

Rietschel, Ernst F. A., 1804–1861
Martin Luther, [1868], Cast 1921–1922
10'
Poehler Building, Concordia College
cast iron
Mr. and Mrs. Ernest Rubbert

Roghair, Dennis, b1953
Grizzly Bear, 1991
8'
MSF entrance, Commonwealth Avenue
elm, chainsaw
Minnesota State Fair Association

Roghair, Dennis, b1953
Anticipation, 1991
5'
MSF Giant Slide, Nelson Street
elm, chainsaw
Minnesota State Fair Association

Roghair, Dennis, b1953
From His Bounty, 1991
7'
MSF Food Building, Underwood Avenue
elm, chainsaw
Minnesota State Fair Association

Roghair, Dennis, b1953
Three Bears, 1991
12'
Red Balloon Bookstore, 891 Grand Avenue
elm, chainsaw
Red Balloon Bookstore

Roghair, Dennis, b1953
Gonna Ride, 1991
8' 5"
MSF Horse Barn, Liggett Street
elm, chainsaw
Minnesota State Fair Association

Rood, John, 1902–1974
Bridgman Court, 1953
90" x 300" x 30"
Bridgman Court, Hamline University
cast stone
Donald Bridgman and Dorothy B. Atkinson
Rood

Sabean, Samuel, b1902
Prancing Horses [two reliefs], 1937
2' x 4' each
MSF Horse Barn, Judson Avenue
cast stone
WPA

Sabean, Samuel, b1902
Poultry [two reliefs], 1937
2' x 4' each
MSF Poultry Barn, Judson Avenue
cast stone
WPA

Shumaker, Gordon, b1920
Pioneer Woman, 1959
36'
MSF Pioneers Building, Underwood Street
fiberglass
Minnesota State Fair Association

Shumaker, Gordon, b1920
Gopher, 1966
24'
MSF Bandshell, Cosgrove Street
fiberglass
Minnesota State Fair Association

Siewert, Betty
Don, 1982
3'
Primate House, Como Zoo
bronze
Artist

Sosin, Georgette, b1934
Sky, 1981
12'
Kellogg and St. Peter Avenues
aluminum
Zonta Club

Stillman, Bruce, b1958
[Untitled], 1987
various
Temple of Aaron Sculpture Garden
steel, painted
Temple of Aaron

St-Gaudens, Louis, 1854–1913
New York Eagle, 1891, m1971

10'
Jackson and 4th Streets
bronze
New York Life Insurance Company

Sugarman, George, b1912
St. Paul Sculptural Complex, 1971
40' x 32' x 29'
First National Bank, 5th & Minnesota Streets
aluminum, steel
First National Bank

Swanson, Bernard, 1910–1977
Santa Claus Town, ca. 1954, m1960
various
Highway 61 and Carver Road
cement
Artist

Swearer, Nick
Iguana, 1978
L 40'
Science Museum entrance, 10th and Cedar
railroad spikes
Science Museum of Minnesota

Tanavoli, Parviz, b1937
Heech, 1971
11'
Student Center, Hamline University
stainless steel
Abby Weed Grey

Taschner, Ignatius, 1871–1913
Johann Friedrich von Schiller, 1907
10'
Como Park
bronze
Schiller Monument Committee

Vogt, Russell
Birdbath, 1989
3'
Temple of Aaron Sculpture Garden
mosaic and cement
Temple

Yasko, Carol, and others
Sisterworks, 1985
various
Oneida, Fort Road and Jefferson Streets
concrete
West 7th Street Federation

St. Peter

Artist Unknown
Elephant [Engresser tomb], 1962
2'

Greenhill Cemetery, Sunrise Drive
cement, painted
Engresser family

Granlund, Paul, b1925
Southwind II, 1982
42″
Gustavus Adolphus College Sculpture Garden
bronze
Rud Lawson Memorial Committee

Granlund, Paul, b1925
Luna Moth Matrix, 1979
60′
Gustavus Adolphus Campus, East Mall
bronze
Douglas Sandberg Memorial Committee

Granlund, Paul, b1925
Apogee, 1980
6′ 2″
Gustavus Adolphus Campus, Eckmann Mall
bronze
Philip and James Lindau families

Granlund, Paul, b1925
Carl von Linne, 1988
3′
Gustavus Adolphus Campus Arboretum
bronze
n.a.

Granlund, Paul, b1925
Masks of the Muse, 1971
72″
Gustavus Adolphus Campus, Anderson Theatre
bronze
Evelyn Anderson

Granlund, Paul, b1925
Venus Nautilus, 1986
33″
Gustavus Adolphus Campus
bronze
Karen Gibbs Memorial Committee

Granlund, Paul, b1925
Joseph - Nicolas Nicollet, 1986
48″
Gustavus Adolphus Campus, Uhler Hall
bronze
Melva Laird

Granlund, Paul, b1925
Jacob and the Angel, 1962
63″
Gustavus Adolphus Campus, Vickner Hall
bronze

College

Granlund, Paul, b1925
BC AD, 1973
48″ cube
Gustavus Adolphus Campus, Bernadotte
    Memorial Library
bronze
College

Granlund, Paul, b1925
Palindrome, 1976
60″
Gustavus Adolphus Campus, Eckmann Mall
bronze
Melvin Hammerberg Memorial Committee

Granlund, Paul, b1925
Crucifixion, 1964
60″
Gustavus Adolphus Campus, East Mall
bronze
Edward and Patricia Lindell

Milles, Carl, 1875–1955
Sun Glitter, [1918], 1982
2′ 7″
Gustavus Adolphus College Sculpture Garden
bronze
Paul and Edna Granlund

O'Connor, Andrew J., Jr., 1874–1941
John Albert Johnson Memorial, 1913
9′
Nicollet County Court House
bronze
Johnson Memorial Committee

Von der Putt, Hans
Gustavus Adolphus (c1632), 1932
2′ 6″
Gustavus Adolphus College
bronze
Frederique and Erik Dahlberg Fund

Staples

Mott Iron Works, J. L.
Soldiers and Sailors Memorial, 1918
25′
Evergreen Hill Cemetery
cast iron, granite
WRC, G.A.R.

Starbuck

Artist Unknown
Star Buck, pre 1972

6′
Minnewaska Home, 7th and Main Streets
concrete
Bill Torgerson

F.A.S.T. Corp.
Hobo, 1987
8′
Hobo Park, Highway 71
fiberglass
City of Starbuck

Kurtz, Mark, b1969
Gnomes, 1990
various
The Gift Cottage, Main Street
wood, chainsaw, paint
The Gift Cottage

Stillwater

Artist Unknown
Samuel Bloomer Monument, 1917
15′
Fairview Cemetery
bronze
Bloomer family

Kohlhagen, C.
Soldiers and Sailors Memorial, 1917
8′
Old Court House, West Pine and 4th Streets
bronze on granite
Citizens of Washington County

Thief River Falls

Creative Displays
Chief Mon-si-moh [or, Red Robe], 1976
15′
Park, Centennial Drive
fiberglass
Thief River Falls Bicentennial Committee

Sears, Stanton, b1950
Falls Thief, 1991
various
Northland Community College
concrete, aluminum
MSAB, Art in Public Places

Tracy

Jaenisch, Steve, b1940
Tornado Tree Monument, 1990
16′
5th Street and Highway 14
steel rods

MSAB, and Chamber of Commerce

Two Harbors

Gage, John, b1951
The Voyageur, 1987
16'
Agate Bay
white pine, chainsaw
Artist

Nelson, Stanley G.
Pierre the Voyageur, 1960
20'
Voyageur Motel, Highway 61
concrete
Voyageur Motel

Sculptured Advertising
Chicken, 1964
8'
Weldon's Gift Shop, Highway 61
fiberglass
Weldon and Marion Johnson

Toth, Peter "Wolf", b1947
Indian Chief, 1977
30'
Tourist Center, Main Street
wood, chainsaw
Artist

Two Inlets

Artist Unknown
Grotto of Our Lady of Lourdes, 1959 to date
various
St. Mary's Catholic Church
concrete, stone, marble
St. Mary's Catholic Church

Vergas

Wegstrom, Ellis, and others
Loon, 1963
20'
West shore of Long Lake
concrete
Vergas Fire Department

Virginia

Martin, Bill
Floating Loon, 1982
20' x 10' x 7' 6"
Olcott Park
fiberglass
Land of the Loon Festival Committee

Wabasha

Poss, John b1933
Skipper
4'
Riverfront
elm, chainsaw
n.a

Poss, John b1933
Missionary, 1987
4'
Riverfront
elm, chainsaw
n.a.

Smit, Jim
Eagle and Wabasha Sign, 1990
12'
Lawrence Blvd. East and Pembroke
wood, chainsaw, paint
City of Wabasha

Waconia

Monumental Bronze Company
Soldiers and Sailors Memorial, 1892
20'
Park, 1st and South Pine Streets
bronze
Various G.A.R. posts

Wadena

Sartell, Chuck
Ice Cream Cone, 1973, m1984
14'
Down Home Foods, Highway 71 north
concrete, painted
Artist

Walker

Artist Unknown
Justicia, 1902, m1961
10'
Cass County Museum, Michigan Avenue
bronze
Cass County

Faber, Jerry, b1934
War Memorial Eagle, 1991
8'
Information Center, Michigan Avenue
wood, chainsaw, paint
Artist

Faber, Jerry, b1934

Welcome Eagle, 1989
10'
Information Center, Michigan Avenue
wood, chainsaw
Artist

Faber, Jerry, b1934
Ernie Eelpout, 1987
7'
Information Center, Michigan Avenue
wood, chainsaw, painted
Artist

Faber, Jerry, b1934
Sea Captain, 1987
7'
Community Health Clinic
wood, chainsaw, paint
Artist

Wayzata

Heffelfinger, Mark, 1947–1986
Ashoka, 1978
5' x 15'
Minnetonka Center for the Arts
stainless steel
Minneapolis Arts Commission

Hunter, John, b1950
The Wizard
12'
244 Wayzata Blvd.
wood, chainsaw
Private owner

Wheaton

Bruns, Robert, b1921
Mallard, 1960
26'
Highway 75, south of city
concrete, steel, paint
Chamber of Commerce

White Bear Lake

Monumental Bronze Company
Soldiers and Sailors Memorial, 1913
21' 5"
Clark Avenue near 2nd Street
white bronze, granite
E. B. Gibbs Post 76, G.A.R.

Shumaker, Gordon, b1920
Polar Bear, 1964, m1989
35'
Thane Hawkins Polar Chevrolet, Highway 61

fiberglass
Thane Hawkins Polar Chevrolet

Willernie

Lutter, A. J.
Bear, 1990
15′
Millner Park
oak, chainsaw
Willernie City Council, Tilton Equipment
    Company

Lutter, A. J.
Eagle, Beaver, and Fish, 1990
15′
Millner Park
oak, chainsaw
Willernie City Council, Tilton Equipment
    Company

Willmar

Holen, Norman D., b1937
Christ and the Child, 1980
25′ x 1′ 6″ x 1′ 8″
Vinji Lutheran Church
terra cotta
Church

Johnson, Robert, b1922
Chief Kandiyohi, 1956, m1983
17′
Kandiyohi County Court House
fiberglass
First American Bank and Trust Company

Sabean, Samuel, b1902
Three Reliefs, 1935–1936
18′ x 6′ each
War Memorial Auditorium, Litchfield Avenue
    and 6th Street W.
cast stone
WPA

Winger

Konikson, Ernie, 1907–1977
Polar Bear and Seal, c1970
3′ 6″
Mobil Station, Highway 59
concrete, paint
Private owner

Winona

Kimball, Isabel Moore, 1863–1950
Princess Wenonah, 1902, m1977

6′
Plaza Mall, 3rd and Center Streets
bronze
W. J. Landon

Sternal, Thomas
Untitled [WSU Torch and letter "W"], 1982
6′
Winona State University Mall
Winona stone
Artist

Winthrop

Bassett, George, b1929
The Harvest, 1983
8′
Main Street, by City Hall
bronze
Winthrop Centennial Committee

Worthington

Lofquist, Janet, b1952
Habitat, 1990
various
Rest & Travel Information Center, Highway 60
dolomite limestone, cast bronze, Cor-ten steel
MSAB, Art in Public Places

Index